"Well, of course! Leave it to Margaret Randall to give us something brand new, something necessary, something that will definitely help us to deal—better than we thought we could."

—June Jordan

"The Price You Pay may be Randall's best book ever. It is rich and intelligent, alive with personality and history, and written with a great deal of compassion and analytical insight."

—John Nichols

"Margaret Randall's books have challenged, educated, and empowered us for decades. In The Price You Pay she leaves the revolutionary countries that inspired Cuban Women Now and Sandino's Daughters and investigates a struggle for liberation closer to home: our need as women to free ourselves from an ignorance about money that tyrannizes us. As always, her work leaves us wiser and stronger. Randall is an essential writer whose work must be read to more fully understand life in these Americas."

— Alice Walker

"A pioneering work of social analysis and a fascinating personal story of the relationship of women to still another master–money. I believe that men as well as women will gain valuable insights from this work."

— Howard Zinn

The Price You Pay

The Price You Pay

The Hidden Cost of Women's Relationship to Money

Margaret Randall

Routledge
New York and London

Published in 1996 by
Routledge
29 West 35th Street
New York, NY 10001

Published in Great Britain in 1996 by
Routledge
11 New Fetter Lane
London EC4P 4EE

Printed in the United States of America
Design: Jack Donner

Library of Congress Cataloging-in-Publication Data
Randall, Margaret, 1936 –
    The price you pay : the hidden cost of women's relationship to money / Margaret Randall.
    p.   cm.
    ISBN 0–415–91203–2 (cloth). — ISBN 0–415–91204–0 (pbk.).
    1. Women—Finance, Personal. I. Title.
HG179.R316 1996
332'024'042—dc20   95–50497

To the memory of my father
John Randall: 1906–1994

the pain you inherited and passed on,
your loving generosity.

Contents

Acknowledgments

I want to thank a number of people whose help in researching and writing this book has been important. More women than I expected took time and energy from busy schedules to sit down with my questions and share intimate, sometimes painful, aspects of their lives. To them, and to all those who have engaged in money talk with me, my heartfelt thanks.

This is the second time I have had the pleasure of working with Marlie Wasserman, my editor at Routledge. Marlie was at Rutgers when I wrote *Sandino's Daughters Revisited*; her wisdom and encouragement always make a better book. When Marlie left Routledge, Kimberly Herald took over; my gratitude also to her and to Mary Carol DeZutter. My agent, Susan Herner, believed in this project when most others didn't quite understand what I had in mind. She continues to be a ready source of strength.

My youngest daughter, Ana, was the first of my offspring to confront me about my own emotional baggage, the strings I frequently attached to money I thought I was offering freely. Our explorations of how this made her feel prodded me to look further at how I felt about the ways in which money was handled in my family of origin, and to ask the early questions that eventually produced so many others. This book also provided the context for a leap in our ability to move with one another through discomfort to understanding. Before the process it unleashed, Chapter 7 would not have been what it is. Thank you, Ana, for helping us come full circle.

My father and mother were also willing to talk about the role of money in their respective families, and, consciously or not, they provided valuable insights. Mother also spent many hours helping me read proof, for which I'm always grateful. My brother, sister, and several friends read the manuscript at various stages, and all offered useful commentary. My partner, Barbara Byers, read innumerable drafts. As always, she discussed, listened, challenged, commented, offered critical feedback, and gave the support she offers in every area of our relationship. She is my best critic.

We count objects. Half of the pictures
will go on your walls, your mother's pottery
is yours. You will need a table, a few chairs
and a bed. My father's books are mine.
We perform dispersion, we transplant
our inherited goods, we are
kings of extravagant calm, Solomons
trying to divide justly.

But the weather is here. New snow crowds
our windows. The woodman came today.
I sent him away. The last of our logs whistle.
After the dead are dead,
fingernails and hair keep growing. I wait
near whatever cannot be divided.

                                        —Jacqueline Frank

Words of Warning
or How I Came to Write This Book

> Somewhere, on the edge of consciousness there is what I call a mythical norm, which each one of us within our hearts knows "that is not me." In America, this norm is usually defined as white, thin, male, young, heterosexual, Christian, and financially secure. It is with this mythical norm that the trappings of power reside.
>
> —Audre Lorde

> Money is never simple. It is real in and of itself, and it is also thick with meaning.
>
> —Carol Ascher

In order to effectively reverse the centuries-old paradigm of male = ownership = control, versus female = dependence = powerlessness, we must begin to deal with the ways women have been made to *feel* about money. We must look at the ruses and regulations by which we have been denied the right to earn it, how our spending continues to be shaped by rules of created need, and how we are urged—always—to look to men for expert guidance in its management. We must also explore the hidden connections between our feelings of money helplessness and our history of abuse.

We need to develop new strategies for thinking about what our relationship to money once was, how it has changed, and what it may become. This book is an exploration of this subtext, the feelings of fear, timidity, helplessness, false loyalties, ignorance, envy, guilt, shame, arrogance, dissociation, and desperation. It is also a look to the future, to a growing realization of ownership and the responsibility that comes with ownership.

My own interest in women and money increased dramatically when I was asked to take charge of my parents' finances at the beginning of the nineties. My father had always earned and handled the money in our family, although we siblings later came to understand that most decisions about money and everything else were Mother's—however camouflaged.

Ours was not an overly secretive household. Yet we (a younger sister, brother, and I—the oldest) had never been told about our parents' economic situation. On the contrary, we were given to believe there was less than there was, that hardship might be just around the corner, that "a penny saved was a penny earned." Much less were we trained in the handling of our family's money. This was especially true for the girls, though our brother was also surreptitiously given the message that business matters were somehow beneath us: lower-class or dirty.

Now my father was beginning to lose his faculties. First he forgot how to subtract, then how to add. He had trouble remembering simple procedures like telling time; hesitated over matters such as deciding how much to give to a particular charity, balancing his checkbook, even writing a check. This left him uneasy and confused. Looking back, I realize how courageous he was as he asked for help.

Soon Dad's attention span grew shorter. He displayed a growing bewilderment. I was careful to help him preserve his sense of participation. Every Monday morning at ten—Dad liked order, resisted change—he would come down the Chamisa- and Cholla-covered hill, the block that separated his house from the one I share with my partner, Barbara. In his hands he carried a small, blue, plastic fishing-tackle box she had given him; "the little blue box," he would say, with his gentle smile. That box was filled with the week's bills, receipts, requests. Later it would also contain a slip of paper on which I wrote his and Mother's current bank balance, for him to refer to if he forgot what it was. Together we would go over his accounts. Gradually I made more of the decisions, my father gratefully looking on. Although denial prevented any of us from naming it back then, we'd begun to suspect he was suffering from Alzheimer's Disease.

We all tried to get my mother to sit in on these weekly sessions, "just in case." She came, rather reluctantly, but stuck firmly to her position that she couldn't understand this sort of thing. While maintaining control of most other family decisions, she had completely internalized the assumption that women like herself just couldn't deal with money.

During my father's three remaining years of life, and since, I have continued to manage his and my mother's financial affairs. The task required self-fashioned courses in accounting, tax law, insurance, stocks, bonds, and cash flow; things about which I had not been taught, and in fact had somehow been given to understand were unnecessary or uninteresting—especially for a girl. It was presumed, after all, that I would marry and a man would take care of such matters.

My life never did line up with the social expectations of my class and time. Long before coming out as a lesbian in my late forties, I moved through a series of relationships with men who understood less about money matters than I did, and certainly earned less. I raised four children with very little financial help from their fathers. I also lived for most of my children's growing-up years and much of my own adulthood in Cuba and Nicaragua, socialist or revolutionary societies where money meant something quite different from what it means under capitalism. At the time this was a relief—so much that should be the right of every human was underwritten by the State. Later my lack of financial savvy would prove an initial impediment to my grasp of my parents' affairs.

At the beginning, as I grappled with their weekly accounts, I sometimes became impatient and even angry, realizing how totally in the dark I had been kept, how little I knew. But I learned fast. I quickly found new professionals to serve my parents' needs; their lawyer, broker, insurance provider, and tax preparer were all either too expensive or inept, and in one case clearly dishonest.

This experience, with all its ramifications, pushed me to think about the ordinary citizen and his or her relationship to money; in particular, the ways in which women are socialized and the place financial trauma occupies in our lives. I wasn't as interested in how women might learn to access or manage money as I was in the feelings that accompany having or being deprived of it, those long shadows cast in childhood that continue to shroud us as we grow. I wanted to explore our inheritance of fears, displacements, the living power of symbols. When I realized that for several years I had been obsessed with the subtext of women and money in the contemporary United States, I decided to write this book.

I started by sending a brief questionnaire to 830 women. I mentioned the lies, secrets, and silences that have traditionally surrounded all our difficult subjects: abuse, food and body-image, self-worth, sex—and also money. I chose my sample from among as diverse a list as possible: women from poor, immigrant, working class, middle- and upper-middle-class, and wealthy families of origin. Women whose class status—as often happens here—had changed dramatically over the years, and those whose position has remained more or less stable. African Americans, Latina and Chicana women, American Indians, Asian Americans, and women from other racial or ethnic backgrounds. Women in their eighties and nineties all the way down to students just emerging from high school or college. Women of varying abilities and disabilities. I was most interested in hearing the stories of grandmothers, mothers and daughters, of lesbian couples, of women in business together.

I accompanied my questions with a letter explaining that I was writing a book about women and money and that I was particularly intrigued by the hidden meaning of money in their lives. I told those I asked to share their stories, thoughts, and feelings and said that I might use their answers to expand my own thinking on the issues, look for common concerns and trends, quote anonymously, or serve as a possible prelude to a more in-depth personal interview. In the course of my research, 37 of these initial questionnaires grew into longer and more detailed conversations. I also spoke informally with dozens of other women.

We're still talking.

Written responses came from 142 women, roughly 11 percent of my list. Unfortunately, my respondents' class, race, and age distribution didn't match that of my initial selection. Considerably more women who had been born into lower middle-class or working-class families and had raised their status by becoming professionals—many of them Jewish—were willing (even eager) to tell their stories. These women were conscious of, and seemed interested in, examining the forces that shaped them. Proportionally more white women responded than women of color. A notably higher percentage of women from immigrant families were interested in exploring their money histories. Conscious feminists—women accustomed to some degree of critical self-examination—were also more likely to take the time to return the questionnaire. Only about a dozen very wealthy women answered, and a small number of women living in poverty.

In asking women to explore and speak honestly about their relationship to money, I also ran into two extremes. On the one hand, several women with whom I'd spoken about my project and who early on showed a good deal of interest ultimately failed to respond. It was clearly a difficult subject, one that brought up all sorts of unexpected—perhaps unwelcome—emotions. A few said they were involved in working on other issues and couldn't shift their attention just now. Some simply remained silent.

One friend who didn't respond seemed surprised when I reminded her of the questionnaire: "Oh," she said, "did you want me to *answer* that? I put it with my stack of bills, and then never got around to it!" Another said she had it somewhere in her office, then quickly changed the subject. Only one friend responded at length, then decided she felt uncomfortable with my quoting her, even anonymously.

On the other hand, a larger number than I expected expressed real excitement. These women thanked me for the opportunity to think about the issue and said it had proved important to them beyond my questionnaire. They spoke of useful discussions with loved ones, a new understanding of habits and attitudes, and in some cases told me, "your questions came at just the right time." Respondents in their forties and fifties were prominent among this group. One woman sent in her answers with a brief note: "This was painful. And fun!" I felt increasingly reaffirmed in my conviction that the underbelly of women and money is a subject whose time has come.

This may have some significance: a few women quickly responded with excitement about my project and included a list of names and addresses of others to whom they said they'd sent my questionnaire. Although they promised their own responses soon, these never materialized. I wonder about the pain that laces these particular money histories and see a parallel with survivors who are able to speak, for example, about another's experience with incest—or incest in general—but are still bound to silence about their own.

In this book attitudes are more interesting than ledgers, and not only those that are evident in the roles money plays in a variety of women's lives. Thought-provoking attitudes also come through in *how* the stories are told or withheld. One respondent, a poet and translator in her forties, defines money as "a subject so painful that I put away the questionnaire and do not have it at hand . . . [but] the least I can do is give you the grim overview of remembered things and present devices."

I have given fictitious names to most of the respondents and others they mention in their narrations while accurately identifying class, age, and racial, professional, or other characteristics. Only with those who specifically requested they be identified, or who are well-known and would have been difficult to disguise, have I retained a public persona, in such cases using a real first name only. Quotes from the questionnaires and/or conversations are included in these ways.

In writing this book I have learned a great deal. I have seen how fluid class is, particularly for women. The mother of one of my narrators sent her, as a child, to the family dentist with two or three dollars in her pocket. "Tell him not to do what you don't absolutely need" were her accompanying instructions. Thirty years later, the daughter is a tenured professor at a major university. Another, born into Hollywood wealth, was forced to declare bankruptcy in her early twenties. She paid off every debt. Later, stronger and more in touch with her own personhood, she returned to the fold of her family's financial security. Another woman, whose life appeared ordinary until circumstances any of us might suffer conspired to put her on the street, is now among the homeless.

Through my explorations, certain experiences surfaced repeatedly, prodding me to return to fundamental questions. How many of my narrators value independence over being cared for, yet have in one way or another been socialized into dependency? Surely a majority. How many feel shame or guilt about our relationship to money? All of us to some degree.

Readers will note that statistics about and testimony from men are entirely absent from this book. Let me say that I do believe our various socializations damage men as they do women. And I know many men who have important things to say about money in their lives, as well as about how their economic conditioning affects their relationships with women and with other men. By extension, or in a mirror image (however inexact), much of this text relates to them as well, particularly to those men who inhabit one or more of the categories of "difference": homelessness, poverty, being of an oppressed race or ethnicity, being gay, or being old. But this is intentionally a book of women's voices. What we have to say should be important to men. It is also vital to women ourselves. And we hear rather steadily from men in other venues; the male viewpoint is central to our ideology. It's our turn here.

I believe that money attitudes are among the most formative we experience; so much of who we become or what we do depends not only on its availability but on how it has been given or withheld, and at what cost. Throughout our lives, these attitudes can be extremely volatile. They tend to change more rapidly and perhaps also more erratically than do those about physical looks or security, fears of abandonment or inadequacy, bravado or shyness, dependency or self-esteem.

This seems particularly true where a feminist consciousness intersects with a woman's life, often redirecting it. Then a woman conditioned to seek and hide within a husband's care may awaken one day to find that she is capable of giving birth to the life she desires. Or the girl-child raised in rigidly controlled wealth may become the woman philanthropist whose causes may be anything but traditional. Just as easily and quickly, in the current economy, a teenage mother or a woman alone with several children can discover that all control has slipped from her grasp and find herself on the street.

In our society, patriarchy and capitalism both conspire to keep us warring, often with ourselves. Money easily becomes the tool, or weapon, with which those who have it or have access to it manipulate and render ever more vulnerable those who do not. Money can also become a metaphor for other successes or failures, and the line between trusting ourselves to manage money and trusting ourselves in other ways may slip and blur.

Gender-related issues, such as sexual violence or childhood abuse, affect our ability to trust others or ourselves—with money matters and much else. When we learn early on that we cannot, must not, depend upon those closest to us, the warning is likely to sound throughout our lives. Race, age, sexual identity, and degree of physical or mental ability may also affect our gendered relationship to a given financial situation.

Gender powerfully determines the opportunities we have to earn, often in skewed juxtaposition to our skill and experience. Wherever money touches or fails to touch us, from the time we are little girls, during every phase of our education and professional lives, and of course most frighteningly throughout old age, we are at a palpable disadvantage with regard to men.

In a patriarchy which is pervasively heterosexist, from before we are born every assumption is that we will eventually marry the man who will care for us. In return for this "security," we are trained to forfeit an independent identity, serve our providers, and shape our daily needs so that we do our part in sustaining the consumer society that keeps us forever alienated from our natural strength, color, size, weight, sexual identity, ideas, allegiances, abilities, erotic energy, and desire. We often do these things mechanically, some small voice inside reminding us that neither protector nor "expert" can really be trusted. Hence the cacophony of discordant messages that plague so many women's sense of self.

Money plays a unique role in our society. As our primary means of exchange, it is eminently practical. We earn it by virtue of our labor, expended in measurable increments: hours and years, level of training, seniority, even background or connections. Or a father, mother, husband, or partner earns it for us. We may also inherit it. Or it may be given to us in the form of a prize or grant, often with implicit or explicit strings attached. Of course women do an enormous amount of unpaid work as well. Most shoulder at least one full-time job in the home, more if caring for several children. Aside from being blatantly unfair, this also skews our sense of our labor's worth.

Money buys time, and this equation has important implications in our lives. The lines between women's paid and unpaid work are socially muddled. Many of us never experience time for ourselves, so imbedded in our psyches is the ethic of service to others. Admonitions such as "You're wasting time (money)" or "The clock is ticking" have become explicitly gendered in our society.

But finances also hold a meaning quite apart from the measurable or practical. Our society has a love/hate relationship to money. It worships the manna even as it vehemently denies that it does so. Money is used to tantalize, seduce, influence, maneuver, manipulate, punish, stand in for attention or love, and to reward behaviors or allegiances that are not always healthy—its very use in these ways bespeaks coercive attitudes on the part of those in control.

In other words, money is power, in brutally manifest and also hidden ways.

Feminism—that is to say, women's varied but far-reaching reconnection to our lives, the revival of memory and history that many currently experience—has made it possible for us to see the contradictions, and to some extent factor them into our awareness of world and self. So, although money mostly remains a topic yet to be explored, some women are beginning to look at our relationship to it from a gender-conscious point of view.

Almost without exception, those who responded to my questionnaire displayed a deep *intellectual* or *political* understanding of the gendered inequities around money, and of how discriminatory attitudes affect them. Dealing with the *emotional* residue is clearly more difficult. Yet a surprising number of respondents also explored this terrain. Woman after woman told stories of misuse and manipulation, resulting in insecurities and fears still prominent in their lives. Many of those with children touched upon attitudes inherited from their own childhoods which they have passed on to their offspring. Women from every conceivable class and culture shared attempts to change their relationship to money.

Myths about money are among a family's most closely guarded secrets—any family, from whatever class and from almost every culture. And the small myths of a family reflect the larger societal myths, the stories of which our lives are made. The relationships these myths define become almost indelible: how much, where it comes from, who spends it, who owns the power. Those who control the money tend to manipulate its flow according to their interests. And the reasons behind their decisions can be as complex as the web of taboos and snarl of attitudes that determine how a family lives its interactions: father to mother, husband to wife, parents to children, sibling to sibling, lover to lover, butch to femme, patriarch to extended aunts or mothers-in-law.

Money Talk

1

or The Last Frontier

Though once, in the quiet attention of our CR circles, we confessed the nature of our orgasms, these days, despite our skill with words, our trust . . . only rarely emboldens us to admit our confusion or shame about either making do with little or expanding into the luxurious possibilities that solid incomes bring.

—Carol Ascher

So long as she merely symbolizes power
she is kept helpless and conventional
her true power routed backward
into the past.

—Adrienne Rich

The adage that warns against bringing up sex, politics, or religion is clearly outdated in the context of current social discourse. Except in the most conservative milieus, almost every sort of sexual preference and practice is discussed today, as are issues such as sexual violence, incest, rape, battery, and childhood abuse.

Over the past ten to fifteen years, increasing numbers of women have taken advantage of feminism's most important gift, a working reconnection with the fact that many, if not most of us, have been cruelly abused as children and throughout our lives. Incest. Rape. Battery. The abuse is widespread and damaging enough that we may legitimately call it terrorism of epidemic proportions. Now that we are beginning to recover our voices, we are learning how to speak about this abuse, which is producing a situation of panic for more than a few men of "untarnished reputation."

In naming and coming to terms with this personal and systemic terrorism in our lives, we learn that our "acceptance" of the assault was motivated by one thing and one thing only: we were too young or broken or vulnerable or fragile or out-powered to fight back. We have come to understand, as well, that we didn't deserve what was perpetrated against us, that it wasn't our fault, and, most importantly, that there are things we can do to reclaim our personhood. A variety of feminist therapies are helping us remember, understand, place in clear perspective, and move through or overcome the damage.

This retrieval of memory and this reinvention of a language that would give us back our lives encourages us to organize or reclaim other areas of experience as well: among them, a healthier relationship to money. Shame is an emotion central to the ways in which money is used to manipulate and control and it is vividly reflected in the ways women talk or refuse to talk about the subject. It is the same shame that is present in such abundance in situations of physical or sexual abuse. This reveals itself to be pandemic in the growing incidence of chronic depression, addictions, eating disorders, phobias, and other paralyzing diseases. And shame translates easily into guilt, the feeling that what happened to us was our fault, that we are to blame for our feelings of inadequacy, ignorance, ineptitude, helplessness, even rage.

This retrieval of voice—of self—belongs not only to that relatively small percentage of the female population that claims a feminist consciousness. The media, popular culture, and other influential vehicles, pro or con, have spread the new consciousness among great numbers of women today. True, the publicity is often adverse, ideas and concepts presented partially or twisted, disparaged or trivialized, in an attempt to discredit feminist ideas, but memory is a powerful weapon, perhaps the most powerful of all. When retrieved and unleashed it is impossible to contain.

Many women still reject a feminist terminology. Others are oblivious to its language. Some have been affected by the backlash (religious fundamentalism, the "false memory syndrome," the attacks on choice and affirmative action, and other exploitative attempts to silence us). Today, however, most women in this country live lives that are different because of the ways in which a handful of courageous theoreticians and activists continue to rethink human history and to demand a recognition of our personhood—by society as well as by ourselves. In one way or another, we are speaking out.

Safety in community and the retrieved power of memory are beginning to replace the isolation of shame and silence. We talk much more freely today about sexual abuse, rape, battery, body image, and other previously taboo subjects. Political debate, or what passes for it, is a veritable media event. And even before the recent terrorist rise of the fundamentalist right, religion too had become an acceptable topic. Money remains a much more veiled and difficult subject, a sort of last frontier. Some of us are barely able to say the word, and seldom with regard to our lives.

We talk about money in the abstract; that doesn't seem to be a problem, or a threat to familiar order. We listen to endless public discussion of the national debt, the trade deficit, how much this or that congressional bill will cost, or the billions—even trillions—such and such a venture will require in taxes. Those doing the selling have become experts at explaining that the funds will be forthcoming from one source of revenue or another. Those who object make sure we know we will be charged, that the money will be taken from our personal pockets. And described in this way, without dividing the figure among the number of people affected, the amount is sure to seem appropriately exorbitant. Concepts like billions or trillions are beyond most people's power to imagine. Statistics are meaningless and selective or incomplete—often used to support whatever thesis is being pushed.

Presidential candidates make solemn promises not to raise taxes, then once in office, find they have "no choice." A multibillionaire independent hopeful like Ross Perot spends personal millions showing graphs and pie charts on television, exploiting a populist line belied by his own business history. Democratic political candidates accuse Republicans of "trickle-down economics." Republican candidates accuse Democrats of "tax and spend," then con a voting public to landslide support with promises of "putting money back in our pockets." We've heard it all before, and experience—memory—should tell us none of it is true. Yet, in ignorance and desperation, we believe.

We should not blame the ordinary American woman for her ignorance any more than for her desperation. A willful decimation of memory has made our conditioning that much easier. Contemporary technology plays mind tricks on us as difficult to decipher and outwit as those older brainwashing techniques, which at least did not pose as something they were not. Still, it is important to understand that the rhetoric means something quite different from what it says. We internalize the official talk, and the routine way in which money is manipulated and lied about in political discourse necessarily impacts the way we are made to feel we must lie about it in our personal lives. A dialectic is created, and the dynamic undoubtedly moves in both directions.

Presentation of information or disinformation is "formatted" by today's media, that is, it is arranged in such a way that our receptive faculties will leap to make the intended connections, while avoiding the consideration of alternatives more likely to be of use. The human mind is literally treated as a computer disk, which must be formatted (electronically prepared) before it is able to receive the information it is given.

In a recent ABC newscast, for example, a paid economist announced that unless our older population gives up Medicare, when they enter the work force babies born today will be burdened by an income tax expected to be 84% of what they earn. It is the fault of our aged, this "expert" claimed, that today's children have no financial future. Nowhere in the segment was our exaggerated defense spending or the huge tax loopholes for corporations mentioned as excessive. Viewers were given no choice but to believe that the poverty-stricken youth of the future are the exclusive responsibility of today's greedy old people who insist on adequate healthcare. This kind of formatting shapes the way we see our relationship to money, in the private as well as in the public spheres.

One of the things we have a great deal of trouble doing is talking about money specifics—down home and personal. Particularly in the smaller human configurations: within the family, in our most intimate relationships, between parents and children, among friends. Fear and insecurity take over, and we seek refuge in learned formulae. Throughout this book, women admit to the routine lies they tell about how much they earn or have, or about what something costs. In its final chapter, I explore how money in my own family of origin was lied about—every expenditure roughly cut in half—and why I think this was. I examine how that tradition became a fixture in my own unconscious, refined and passed on to my children until at least one of them rebelled.

It is much easier, in today's United States and across class and cultural lines, to talk about sex, religion, or politics, than it is to truthfully tell one another how much we earn, need, spend, save, have—about how certain monetary customs hurt us, about the shame we were made to feel as children if we "cost too much." Or the shame we feel as adults because we have too little or too much; or because we lack control over what we have. Because we have been manipulated by power wielded through money. Because we manipulate others, using money as bait or as a currency of domination.

Whatever their class status, parents rarely talk with their offspring about money. Or, they may talk, but not honestly. Children generally grow up ignorant of their parents' finances. In most middle- or upper-middle-class heterosexual unions, husbands frequently handle all money matters; wives often become widows unaware of what they can rely upon. Worse, when they are widowed they may be left not knowing how to balance a checkbook, pay bills, file tax forms, or any of the other tasks their husbands took care of for them both.

It is not only our money talk that is distorted or silenced. Ours is also a society unaccustomed to speaking about economic class, and untrained for the task. Because of the way our land was colonized and how its industrialization and social development unfolded, mobility between classes is somewhat easier and more common in the United States than it is in other countries. But there are also more myths. In a nation with vast differences between the very wealthy and a growing homeless population, almost everyone—if asked—would define themselves as middle class. Yet the tag means something different to almost all who use it. Politicians and commentators, in their frantic efforts to protect privilege, have taught us a double-speak that leads to a failure of meaning. Little is spoken about as it is.

In fact, the United States has produced a confusion of class and race—the first mutable, the second usually not—that is particularly U.S. and particularly twentieth century. In most of my narrators' stories, a woman's sense of self-worth is directly traceable to how much money there was in her family of origin, how her relationship to it was perceived and handled, and what attitudes about it she developed. But class today means something much more complex than one's financial origins or current status. It is important to understand how all the variables intersect.

Twentieth-century U.S. society has long distorted traditional class lines. Certain highly paid tradespeople, underpaid teachers, intellectuals, and artists stretch the meaning of class in different directions. More important, with the information revolution computers are replacing human workers in greater and greater numbers. In this era of massive layoffs, "downsizing," and other disguised disemployment, a person's relationship to production gains in importance. Those who own the means of production may survive—for as long as there are buyers for what they produce. Those who must sell their labor run an increased risk that their source of income will suddenly be taken from them.

And so for the first time in history, the person earning $70,000 may be in as much danger of sudden poverty as the person earning $12,000. Not true, you may say, because in the event of job loss the person earning $70,000 will surely have put some money aside. But the handling of personal finances rarely follows such a logical pattern. Most people live at the edge of their income or beyond; their language reflects the disparities: "My credit card is maxed to the limit." "I spend faster than I earn." The loss of a job always comes as a shock. This puts a new spin on economic class. And it is a situation particularly threatening to women, who have long been treated as a reserve labor force despite the fact that we currently support almost half the nation's families.

Neither is class only or primarily defined by family income or inherited wealth; it also reflects culture, education, race and racial stereotypes, gender, age, sexual identity, choice, a proclivity to risk, natural disaster, contingency, even luck. What differences do we experience if our money is earned or inherited? If there is someone we may go to for help, or nothing or no one to fall back on? If we are outside the vaguely delineated middle class? If we are single? If we are gay? If we are differently abled? If we are black? If the street is our home? How do these disparate conditions affect how we talk about money, or if we talk about it at all?

Those born into affluence or for whom having money has come easily may claim it as a means of exchange with no awkward or uncomfortable implications. It's the norm. Neutral. As American as apple pie. "Well, we're off to Bermuda for the weekend!" Certainly no cause for embarrassment or shame. Yet these women's language often reflects discomfort with what they have, and a deeper look into their lives may reveal a subterranean dis-ease. The way our system protects the haves and pits them against the have-nots conditions and perpetuates unhealthy relationships on all sides.

Those born into poverty, on the other hand, who have grown up witnessing loved ones struggling or sacrificing to provide for basic needs—and those whose hard work may not have been *enough* to provide for basic needs—are more likely to feel that money is synonymous with value or worth. "I'm really no good at this . . . always behind . . . can't manage to get caught up . . . don't know how I'll ever make it." For those who have known poverty, it may always remain difficult to separate how much they have from who they believe they are.

Then there is the effect of social misnaming. How often do poor white women describe themselves as middle class—because according to every media message and social indicator, America itself *is* middle class, and white? This, we have been taught, is the great melting pot. But to melt successfully we must conform to the dominant image: have white skin and reproductive sexual habits, worship as a protestant, inhabit a diminishing shape and size, take on what are presumed to be male characteristics in business or politics, display the right amount of humility (or its flip side, sexual come-on), marry and produce 2.3 children, and enjoy an acceptable economic status. This is where class (itself a complex category, as we've seen) intersects with a host of other variables to tell us who we are permitted to be. In an era of highly sophisticated, often subliminal signals, until we are able to hone our consciousness, the projected image—however false—may *feel* more real than actual experience.

Chaia Lehrer offers a vivid picture of how a family's class can fragment, by describing in almost biblical detail the complex way in which her own set itself up for the pain and loss of generations of divisions. In a piece called "Those Old Working Class Values,"[1] she pictures her uncle's funeral. The family configuration, the way relatives treat one another, clarify the ways money and gender intersect to produce the class hierarchy in which the author was raised. Listen to the naming of categories situating family members along a scale of immutable positions:

"My mother was one of five children," she begins, remembering her grandmother crying because she had no food for her children, her uncles sleeping on wooden chairs pushed together.

> By the time I was born, everyone had fallen into place within a hierarchy. My uncle who died took top position when he married a woman with some family money and a ruthless zeal to get a lot

more. Their children, my cousins, became upper middle class. My mother's sister married a man with a college degree who worked as a store manager. They took second place and their children became upper middle class. Next was my uncle, a postal worker, who married a woman without money, but because he was a man and had a son as well as a daughter, he took position three. Their son became middle class, and their daughter remained working class. My mother took fourth place when she married a "laborer," as she referred to my father, and they had three daughters. Two of us remained working class, one is lower middle class. Last place was another uncle who married a poor woman and had a differently-abled son and two daughters. This family was unable to socialize in many ways and was ostracized.

Lehrer goes on to talk about how, at the funeral, the older generation mingles and shows some respect for one another and for their offspring; but the behavior of the younger generation—her cousins—conforms to this rigidly established hierarchy. Those at the top socialize with one another. Those at the bottom vie, without success, for the attention of those at the top. The "last place" family isn't even invited. And her own family is barely spoken to.

By the time those who have suffered this sort of stigmatization based on perceived or real class position find their own niche, a negative sense of identification may be set for life. Parents may make it uncomfortable for children to date or marry outside their class or culture. Girls are often urged to "marry well," meaning a man with more money or better job prospects. The North American fervor about working one's way up frequently takes over. Cross-class association is discouraged. And values not associated with wealth are tacitly disparaged.

At the same time, in this country it is common for young women, even young women from the middle and upper-middle classes, to work at all manner of temporary jobs—waiting tables, cleaning houses, as nannies, or secretaries—to make extra spending money to get through school, help a spouse, or even, when still young, to "learn the value of money." Such scenarios are unheard of among their counterparts in most other countries, where class is much more structured and divisions more rigidly held.

And then there is that intentional blurring of class lines that muddles the interests of those who fall victim to this intensely capitalistic phenomenon. It is a blurring that speaks a language of its own. Owners and managers may cheerfully urge their workers "Come on, now, we're all in this together!" We hear service workers and upper management refer to their company's personnel in the first person plural, although the former may bring home six-figure salaries and the latter be dealt a pink slip with neither notice nor compensation. Women are often doubly victimized by this sort of lie, which also coerces us into believing that unrewarded service may keep us employed, that a sexually enticing appearance is more advantageous than education or training, or that we didn't deserve a promotion because, after all, we do have the obligation of that other job to do at home.

In the workplace the myths unfold in multiple and overlapping arenas. Unions have difficulty organizing workers who cannot see where their real interests end and those of their bosses begin. Gender defines a special workplace exploitation and oppression. Women are objectified by male bosses. We are much more likely than men to operate out of an ideology of service and caring, and we also lack male organizing history. Our experience is therefore further manipulated.

There is a great imbalance around job categories, how these are spoken about, and the remuneration they bring. For example, construction, precision tooling, plumbing, and other typically male trades are generally well-paid and are seen as "tough jobs for real men." Woman-friendly job categories such as public school teaching remain grossly underpaid, and although you will hear periodic lip service given to the idea that "we need good teachers," economic and prestige incentives lag far behind. Still, teachers, undervalued and underfunded as they are, tend to think of themselves as professional, and therefore middle class. This false identification is bolstered by a misleading use of terms. The word "professional" opens some doors while closing others.

Salary determines significant difference, not only in the way society views a woman but in the way that a woman views herself. The way we talk about a profession or trade, the language we use, exalts or stigmatizes as well. Job descriptions are important: psychiatrist as compared to psychologist or counselor, doctor as opposed to physician's assistant or nurse, custodian versus janitor, actor versus entertainer, professor versus teacher, person in retail versus sales clerk. The first set of titles refers to positions most frequently held by men, while women typically fill the second.

Women who do not work outside the home are similarly exploited. Their endless hours of household labor go unrecognized and unpaid. If there is a working husband in the picture, a wife may feel protected or even privileged that he "earns enough for both." But in many cases she will also relinquish what decision-making she may have achieved, because he, after all, is "putting the food on the table." Often this woman will not stop to consider that *she* is quite literally putting the food on the table, as well as shopping for and preparing it, cleaning house, washing and ironing the family's clothes, and routinely servicing all other aspects of her husband's and children's daily needs—with no salary for any of this. And when asked what she does, the housewife is likely to answer "nothing." Unpaid and undervalued, her work becomes invisible even to herself.

Women's volunteer work, outside the home as well as in it, is another of the great untabulated and unacknowledged areas of production. In spite of statistics that show increasing numbers of single-parent families,[2] women are *assumed* to be more able to give of their time than men. We are *presumed* more flexible. And we are, of course, more *naturally* willing to volunteer—the old care ethic. Again, our language reflects how we are used: "Of course I'll do what I can." "Here, let me help you with that." "I'll be there; you can count on me."

If a woman is a single mother on welfare, she is usually subject to the rules of a system more interested in its own political agenda than in helping her achieve independence; often she is forced to avoid marrying, or to lie about this and other aspects of her personal situation simply in order to survive. A corrupt system makes sure she *cannot* tell the truth about money.

A single mother, particularly if she is young and undertrained, may take her frustrations out on her child or children; who else is so close at hand? A person for whom a lack of money at a particularly important juncture meant a lack of safety or security, may do anything to make sure she is never without it; while someone who never had to think about money may retain a posture utterly out of step with the demands of a market economy. These attitudes are reflected in the ways both talk about money—or don't.

The feminization of poverty is a direct result of the masculinization of wealth. And as complex as class and gender issues are in sifting through our attitudes about money, race and ethnicity are equally complicated—and relevant. Identity and capability are strongly defined by class or class perception, but they are also affected by race, assumptions based on racial stereotyping, and the perceptions we internalize. How do we experience ourselves if we are Indian, Asian, Latina, Black, or Jewish? Or Arabic in a society that currently equates Middle Eastern heritage with terrorist intent? How is our experience of race fed by—and how does it feed—our relationship to money?

Our country's dominant culture spawns racism like the plague. A black woman is presumed poor. And quite often she is. But what of the woman who is black and comfortable, or even black and wealthy? Perception can be as much of a marker as reality. Not only do others tell us what they think of us through their acceptance or rejection—the barely perceptible gesture, the rude dismissal—but we ourselves internalize the prejudice—with its consequent feelings of lack or loss. And guilt.

How often is an African American (or Indian or Hispanic) person of ample means considered poor by white friends or acquaintances because color is visible and class neither understood nor acknowledged? How often does such an assumption become a core part of the way that person sees herself? One of my narrators, from a large extended African American family, says it happens all the time.

Vinnie is a middle child of seven, with numerous aunts, uncles, cousins. There were few black people in the small Texas town where she was born and grew up, most of them related. Her father had been stationed at the local Air Force base and later put down roots. She says this "uniqueness" cast her childhood as an anomaly, placing racism in a slightly different register. Money was never superfluous; her father's military salary and what her mother earned baking and selling mince pies were the mainstays then. But gradually her older brothers went to work and began to contribute. She cannot remember "going without."

Today, at 27, Vinnie is a technical writer for a large computer company. She earns a comfortable salary,

> more than comfortable since I'm single and don't have to worry about family. I think race and status are linked to money issues [though], in all sorts of ways. People have you typed, you know. When I meet someone I can tell they're thinking, black: lower-

middle class or poor, a disadvantaged childhood at least. . . . It's like they see black, they see woman, but they don't see tech writer with a good job, family that was able to provide an education to seven sons and daughters. All of us who wanted to, got through college. The state school, but still. . . . Two quit to get married. But they're okay. I mean, it's never been about money, not for me. It's about who you are, what people can see of that, and what they won't bother trying to see. . . .

Jews still routinely suffer the stereotype of being viewed as "great business people, greedy, stingy; rulers of the media, government, the world."[3] With the current upsurge in fascist offensive, white supremacist, racist, anti-Semitic, fundamentalist, anti-woman, and anti-gay organizing going on in our country and globally, the money phrase "to Jew a person down" takes on a whole new meaning. Middle- or upper-middle-class Jewish women are often referred to as JAPs, Jewish American Princesses: "controlling rich bitches," in the words of the narrator quoted above. Anti-Semitism, then, may make Jewish women think or feel differently about their relationship to money, regardless of economic worth.

Age is an additional variable. Consider the older woman, her diminishing value as worker or spender. Socially she is perceived as a burden rather than as a source of labor or creativity, or even as a consumer of goods or an object of desire. Her relationship to money is not so clear; she may no longer earn it, or have lost its provider through death or divorce. Even if she has saved astutely or is in a position to care for herself, age trivializes and lessens her worth in society's eyes.

The older woman also becomes the easiest mark for a proliferation of con artists and swindlers. Our media talk shows and human interest segments are filled with desperate tales of the elderly widow who has lost her hard-earned security or the man who has made a profession out of marrying wealthy women. And then there is the woman of any age or income who is made to feel she must *buy* friendship, companionship, even sex—because alone she is both extraordinarily vulnerable and also "half a person."

Sexual harassment more often victimizes younger women, of course— again because of stereotypical perceptions. Older women frequently experience a misplaced sense of relief that they no longer attract the unwanted attention. At whatever age, however, sexual harassment bears directly upon a woman's position in the workplace, her sense of belonging or alienation, her feelings about herself.

What happens to the working woman who knows she must submit to this form of assault from a boss in order to keep a job, pay her bills, feed her family? What happens to a woman who must humiliate herself for years, perhaps with a succession of bosses? What does this do to her self-confidence, to say nothing of her relationship to her labor's worth? Inevitably she herself becomes an object of sale and resale. And a whole other set of feelings and responses enters into the work-for-wages equation.

The language of money is consistently described in terms of *yours*, *mine*, and *ours*. Women are often absent in the *yours*, invisible in the *mine*, and too small a part of the *ours*. Today many states have joint property laws. That is, each member of a heterosexual married couple legally owns one-half of their common property. If the marriage ends in divorce, and roughly half of all legal unions in this country do, what has been accumulated is divided, as well as the responsibility for debts accrued.

Not just the owner class, but many less wealthy couples have begun to design prenuptial agreements—replete with a new sort of money language—in order to protect assets brought into a marriage. Even before they marry, women as well as men are urged to think about the possible dissolution of the partnership. Yet women are still much more likely to emerge from an unsuccessful marriage with far fewer financial assets and a less secure future than our male counterparts. Women suffering from many-layered abuse are often willing to give it all up to escape an unbearable situation.

For lesbian partnerships, legal protection is only beginning to be achieved in a very few localities, while the backlash of the organized right continues to threaten and often overturn such progress. Lesbians, perceived as particularly threatening and therefore hated by the patriarchy, socially unacknowledged and rarely protected by law, earn less than our heterosexual sisters. We pay more for health insurance, cannot file joint tax returns, do not receive our partner's social security check when we survive her, and so carry an added vulnerability to money manipulation. And when we dare to speak the language of our oppression, we are condemned for seeking "special interest" privilege, being obsessive or strident.

Lesbian mothers have the most difficult time with our legal system, followed by underage heterosexual mothers and then single mothers of any age. The very nature of male-controlled society consistently supports the fathers, while rarely holding them accountable. Social analyst Katha Pollitt has pointed out that in a broad range of custody cases these days mothers are most often awarded their children when the fathers don't want them.[4]

Divorced mothers suffer their own financial stress. In the United States they are still more likely to be given custody,[5] but our justice system has proven almost incapable of seeing to it that off-site fathers contribute their fair financial share of child support. June Jordan put it as well as anyone when she wrote:

> According to the law, what a father owes to his child is not serious compared to what a man owes to the bank for a car, or a vacation. Hence, as they say, it is extremely regrettable but nonetheless true that the courts cannot garnish a father's salary, nor freeze his account, nor seize his property on behalf of his children, in our society. Apparently this is because a child is not a car or a couch or a boat.[6]

The attitudes we carry about money are complex: sometimes fluid, sometimes set as a clenched jaw, not always traceable to class, hunger, or affluence alone. And they needn't emanate from our immediate reality. A mother who suffered privations in her youth may make her children feel they are too expensive, even when her new family's income is adequate to its needs. Or she may compromise herself, so that her offspring never have to suffer what she suffered. A father who punishes and rewards with money rather than with warmth, praise, encouragement, surely affects his children's sense of self, and they are likely to repeat the betrayal with their own sons and daughters.

How many women try to make up for failing to measure up to whatever physical standard is in vogue, or for our damaged self-esteem, by wooing with money substitutes: food, favors, unasked-for-help, gifts? Exaggerated gifting is a whole other chapter in the language of money = love. And women seem unusually prone to this practice. Who among us, at one time or another, has not given and given and given—because it made her feel appreciated, or kept her from feeling invisible? Excessive gifting in and of itself is a subtext common to women across class and cultural lines.

And money gets mixed up with two of the other contemporary female danger zones: food and sex, or sexual abuse, which is not about sex but about power. A friend recently described how, in times of stress, she and an ex-lover withheld food and sex from one another, interchangeably. Most of us have stories about eating to quell discomfort or to fill an empty place inside. Or about going on a buying spree to make ourselves feel better about something totally unrelated to material need. In our culture, "shop 'til you drop" is put forth and played to as a female proclivity "natural" to our gender.

Appearance is yet another indicator. It can be as important as class, race, age, or culture in this country's complex coding around women and money. It would be redundant to enter into a discussion of "You are how you dress," the assumption that underlies contemporary fashion. A multi-billion dollar industry depends for its survival and immense profit upon its ability to make American women believe we must change our appearance seasonally: buying what is in, discarding what is out.

Clothing, beauty aids, and makeup, the teaching of "charm," weight-loss programs, and many other subsidiary industries take our money and repay us with the frustration and humiliation of products or programs which do not make the promised difference. Worse, we are left with our own feelings of inadequacy reinforced. And we repeat the language of that inadequacy: "It might have worked, if only I had stuck to it . . . or done it right."

Clothes and appearance are also indelible social markers, proposing to tell others who a woman is, what she is worth. The wealthy woman's understated elegance is perfectly distinguishable from the poor woman's cheap attempts at imitation. There is a role for each, of course, and each is limited by the social expectations inherent in that role. Additionally, the poor woman literally believes she is *worth* less, and frequently cannot even access what she might do to change this. Her money talk perpetuates a lack of self-esteem.

Sports icons, film stars, and the CEOs of major U.S. companies take home six- and seven-digit salaries and additional benefits an ordinary worker finds almost impossible to imagine. Women, of course, are in the extreme minority among those who stash away such monies. And, for women and men who stray from an American as Apple Pie image, the extras are always much more difficult to collect. The tennis pro Martina

Navratilova is a case in point. By anyone's criteria, she is one of the world's great athletes, as well as exceptionally articulate. But her decision not to hide her sexual identity—in fact to speak out for gay rights, freedom of choice, and ecological issues—meant that during her pro career her endorsements diminished.

All this is at the top end of money. At the bottom end, the homeless, who have no income at all, are ever more present on our city streets. A steadily deepening economic crisis pushes more and more people beyond the protection of work-for-wages security. Among them, women and children are increasingly prominent. Ann S. Nihlen, of the University of New Mexico, has been interviewing homeless women and men in Albuquerque over the past several years. Listen to these women's money talk:

> Vivian: I've been homeless for awhile, you know. It started when my car broke down a couple of years ago. And somehow I went over to the Salvation Army. And I got kind of involved with just being on the street and before you know it, I stayed out there and traveled around, you know, and 'course I was drinking a lot, so that was okay. You know, I just didn't care. In the wintertime it's a bitch.
>
> Evelyn: How it happened was my daughter moved in with me with two of my granddaughters and I was the only one working at the time. I did not realize she had a drug problem. She got her check stolen, that I knew for a fact, and it put us way behind. I couldn't pay the rent or anything. Well, they condemned the place where we were at, so we got evicted. . . .
>
> Vivian: As far as like surviving, making money or anything, um . . . 'course I got food stamps, you know, and sometimes they'd sell them, sometimes they wouldn't. Sometimes I'd prostitute, you know, but I don't have to do that anymore. But you do what you have to do, you know. If you go three or four days and you want a drink or you want something else, you got to figure out a way to make money. Someone comes up and offers it to you . . . it's really hard to say no. Don't necessarily go looking for it. It was never a habit of mine. But it was available. I didn't steal.

Does this testimony reflect attitudes unique to society's most disenfranchised? I would argue no. Similar feelings and expressions reproduce in every social class. The situation that defines the problems, how much money we're talking about, the language we employ on its behalf, and how it translates in the living are what differ. Vivian and Evelyn are forced to accept the definitions our system makes available to them. Within those definitions they learn to function as they can. The daily pressure to survive obscures the possibility of alternatives. Focusing down to immediate problems closes the window on a larger vision.

Being coerced or conditioned to focus down is endemic to many women's lives. Too often we are taught to take what is offered, put on a brave face, make do with less than what we want or need. Men, especially idealistic men, often set a standard which equally idealistic women are urged to believe justifies all manner of sacrifice on their part. Not surprisingly, such relationships frequently end with the men displaying dissatisfaction or frustration with the very tyranny they have imposed. The following story is eloquent in this respect. It also offers an example of the money talk typical of a conscious woman who nonetheless has internalized a vocabulary of oppression.

Joan is one of the women who responded to my questionnaire. A psychologist in her fifties, she was one of two daughters of parents of European Jewish descent. She describes her mother as "want[ing] to use money to wield power over me" and her father as eventually being more supportive, "approving of my efforts to find my identity and take the path least traveled, perhaps something he, who had married during the depression years, had never had the opportunity to do." Joan's own marriage was illustrative of many at the time, in which the husband felt free to explore his interests while the wife was forced to support his needs.

But before discussing her marriage Joan reminisces about an early money-related custom in her childhood, one that was linked to the celebration of Chanukah. "Instead of getting gifts from my grandparents," she remembers, "we got Chanukah gelt." The whole family, including many cousins, would come together for a party and Grandpa would bring out rolls of coins. As the children gathered around, he would toss handfuls of these into the air, and the kids would scramble to gather as many as they could. Since Joan and her younger sister were the smallest, they were often outmatched by more able or more practiced cousins. Their grandfather, firmly entrenched in the role of benevolent provider, would slip them a few extra dollars so they wouldn't feel outranked.

Joan speaks of babysitting her younger sister beginning around the age of seven. She was paid 25 cents a night, and her sister received 5 cents "for being well-behaved." Here we have monetary remuneration from a very early age for the female who is good. Later the babysitting jobs extended beyond the immediate family, and there was the usual allowance for school lunches, movies, 45 rpm record hits, and stamps for her collection. By high school there were other after-school jobs, and by Joan's second year of college she had managed a trip to Europe—on saved earnings and many years of money gifts.

High school was the context in which Joan met the man who would be her husband. Much before the legalization of that union, she describes "taking over the responsibility for paying [his and his roommate's] bills" because she "got tired of the electric company threatening to cut off the lights." By this time, she was thoroughly conditioned to take over the part her own mother had played in relation to her father. What Joan has to say about money in her marriage is particularly interesting, not only because it reproduces inherited roles, but because it is typical of so many sixties and seventies couples in which the man proposed living according to certain ideological premises and then begged out—based, at least in part, upon his dissatisfaction with his wife having molded her own life to his ideals:

> When I got married, money or the lack of it was often a problem between us. At first we both were graduate students, living in married student housing. We had to take short-term loans to pay our in-state tuition . . . and then lived from month to month on a graduate assistant's stipend. My husband was something like my father, in that he liked to spend money without thinking about a budget, but he didn't have the income to back it up. I knew 1,001 ways to cook hamburger, and each month struggled with which bill should get paid and which one could be stalled. . . .
>
> Later in our life together, my husband worked at a series of low-paying or nonpaying jobs, as a community or labor union organizer. We had made some decisions about this political commitment being a way to act on our values, and I agreed to be the major breadwinner. This wasn't difficult for me, because I was

finishing graduate school and later working in the profession that I had trained for. In fact, in those days, just as the women's movement was getting started, with the publication of Betty Friedan's book *The Feminine Mystique*, I didn't think I was oppressed as a woman because I was a professional and not tied to my home as a suburban housewife and mother.

Nevertheless, my husband still liked to buy expensive toys, like cameras and motorcycles. (Didn't Dorothy Parker say that the difference between men and boys is the price of their toys?) He charged things on credit cards without concern about how the bill would be paid. For a long time we pooled our income in the same checking account, but would divide the balance between us for daily living and expenses.

As I began to be depressed about my job, I felt burdened by the responsibility to keep working at it, because there were always bills to be paid. My husband and I began to divide our money up in a different way. We still had a joint checking account, but we started two separate savings accounts. One was my husband's "goodies" account, and he agreed to not buy any toys unless there was money in the bank. The other was my "freedom" account, in which money was saved so that eventually I could quit my job without worrying about paying the rent and putting food on the table.

The equating of a man's goodies with a woman's freedom is remarkable here. It is but one of dozens of examples that surfaced among the varied responses to my questionnaire, in which independence or dignity for a woman was contrasted—in her conditioned sense of what partnership should be—by a man's promise not to deprive his family by collecting the toys he continued to feel were his right. In retrospect, Joan is able to understand the situation for what it was:

As you can see, being the main earner for a large part of our marriage didn't give me a lot of power in decision-making. It was only after I was willing to be more assertive and beginning to struggle for equality in the [relationship] that I had a more equal say in our financial affairs. The irony of it is that when our marriage did break up, one of my husband's [stated] reasons for wanting to leave was that *he didn't feel right in his labor organizing to urge co-workers to go on strike when he always had a financial cushion of my income behind him.* (my emphasis)

This story vividly illustrates the subtle and not so subtle ways in which men are socialized to use the women with whom they share their lives, and the money talk they develop to justify such use. This young husband went through school on his wife's paycheck, then found that the "cushion" her work provided was at odds with his political idealism. Easier, I suppose, than having to look at other incompatibilities—for which he might have had to accept some responsibility. Many young women, taught to look to the men in their lives for their philosophical as well as emotional stability, have trouble seeing through this "analysis"—at least when it is initially offered. For years they may add to their original store of guilt the guilt of somehow having failed at "making the marriage work."

Money takes on different roles in our society, depending upon the needs and interests of those in power. Sometimes it is trivialized, sometimes mocked or pretended to be unimportant. More often it is worshipped. More about this in the next chapter. For now, consider the variety of money-making schemes, the equation of salary with prestige, the vast advertising of luxury items, always with the inference that what costs more is worth more (also magically imbuing its owner with certain desirable qualities such as youth, beauty, skills, business or social success, sexual prowess, a loving family, happiness).

Among working-class people in general, and in the old Italian or newer Latina communities in particular, women are much more likely to control household spending. The husband may earn the only or primary salary but, in the smooth-running household, come payday he will turn his check over to his wife. She will cash it. She may give him something back with which to play, and then she will administer the bulk, making sure the most important household expenses are covered. Such an arrangement makes it possible to *pretend* control when none is held. It is a way of talking a line of money management belied by reality.

I have heard numerous working-class women complain about husbands who "can't manage money," even as they expect and nurture the above-mentioned arrangement and would not think of trying to change it. Traditionally, they don't trust men who, left to their own devices, might spend or drink away too much of what they earn. But a part of them enjoys the imagined control while ignoring their total dependence on their husbands and resenting having to keep such tabs on them.

Lolita cleans houses. She is 42, her mother Hispanic, her father of Irish descent. She and her husband (who works at a 7–11 store) have two teenage sons. The combined salaries of both adults averages around $40,000 a year. Lolita is a working-class woman with mixed ethnic and class roots: her family tells stories of field hands around the table on her grandfather's ranch, a sawmill, and land still owned though now inactive. Through financial ups and downs, Lolita has always heeded her grandmother's almost primal warning about husbands: "When you girls marry, be sure and handle the money, and when possible set some aside without your spouses knowing." A woman who has moved considerably from her culture of origin, Lolita nevertheless admits

> I try not to keep any secrets from my husband but sometimes I wish I could tell him that I have some money saved with my name only. When my husband asks me how much money we have in the checking account I'll always tell him much less than there really is. The account's in my name only but both our checks go in there.

There is a very different money-handling tradition in the mostly white middle class, although it also seems to be shaped by generation. Women, particularly those who are currently in their seventies or eighties, didn't complain if they were "taken care of." For most it is what they were raised to expect and conditioned to want. When husbands precede them into death, however (and this is the usual order of things),[7] they are often additionally confused and upset by the fact that they were kept so passive with regard to money management.

As with all generalizations, there are notable exceptions. Like many of the women in this book, Elizabeth, at age 69, has an unusual story to tell. It is one that includes a very different sort of money talk: knowledgeable, confident, exuberant. During her early childhood, her father was the treasurer of a cattle association, sometimes taking the train home from a sale with as much as $10,000 cash in his pocket. He was also a director of their local small-town bank. Elizabeth remembers the crash and subsequent closing of the country's financial institutions:

> I recall the day [my father] came home mid-afternoon carrying a dripping quart of vanilla ice cream which he had bought for us just prior to hearing the news. I couldn't understand what was happening

but I was aware a major event had occurred. I remember hearing him talk about the need to borrow money so he could pay the people who lost theirs. He was the only director in town who did this, and he paid 10 cents on the dollar. I received a dime!

Elizabeth's privileged childhood, which had seemed average to her, changed then. There were fewer vacations to Atlantic City and no more expensive hotels "complete with finger bowls" or diamond and sapphire rings for the asking. Money was less available, but class—in this case the status and access necessary to its acquisition—remained. Her parents were able to borrow money, buy a large house on Main Street, and begin taking in tourists. Elizabeth remembers single rooms costing $1.00, doubles $1.50, lots of sheets to be ironed and folded, and bus trips to Boston to visit grandparents back when pillows could be rented for 25 cents. When she was ten, her father took the real estate exam and became a broker.

I was really intrigued with this, loved being in his office with his two big desks and his sharpened pencils, his day book. I can still hear him telling someone on the telephone about a house which might require $200 down and maybe $35 a month.

Elizabeth's father provided his daughter with a rare contact with the business world, and her fascination with money matters took off. She developed an interest in and a talent for the market, with all its intricacies and complexities. These many years later, she gives back what she can by buying office supplies for her grandchildren, and encouraging their playing at business. She hopes to spark confidence and creativity—especially in her granddaughter. She has also started a small but balanced portfolio for each child, using corporations with which they are familiar: McDonald's, Coke, Boeing.

Despite all his daughter's business acumen, when it was time to appoint an executor for his will Elizabeth's father reverted to tradition and chose a half-brother over her. Her mother championed her full brother who was clearly incapable of handling the estate. Elizabeth's first husband literally battered her where money matters were concerned. Years of struggling for control of her own assets taught her a lot about what a woman's relationship to finances can be. She was married to her first husband for twenty-three years, and describes him as "a total controller" of their funds:

> I was given $600 a month for groceries, dry cleaning, help, the needs of three children—all [the] cash expenditures. If I went over, it would be deducted from the following month's account. I remember that one year on my birthday I requested money towards a chair instead of going out to dinner. He refused. We went out to dinner.

This marriage pushed Elizabeth into therapy, and she recalls her therapist at one point suggesting her husband provide an extra $100 a month that didn't have to be accounted for. "This lasted only a short time," she says, "as I filed for divorce within the year." After eight years alone she married again, and has been with her current husband, now in his mid-eighties, for seventeen years. At the beginning, she had to deal with his financial eccentricities. Then he gave the handling of their affairs completely over to her. She says that for the past decade she has felt comfortable with the arrangement. "I have a diversified, broad-based portfolio of stock and tax-exempt bonds which I manage totally by myself. I do my own research, make my own decisions. I use a discount broker."

All three of Elizabeth's daughters, now 42, 41, and 37, have been or are in therapy. All, she says, have problems dealing realistically with money. Only the oldest has shown an interest in learning what Elizabeth has to teach. She has recently gone into business for herself and uses the profits to build her own portfolio. Elizabeth has named this daughter executor of her will, and has gradually shared with her all necessary information about her assets.

It has been frustrating to Elizabeth that two of her daughters and most women she knows refuse to take control of their money. She says she has seen changes, since her own childhood, but they are slow.

> Many women my age don't want to know. I've tried to educate them, and it saddens and angers me when a friend will say: "But I have the nicest trust officer; he takes me to lunch and we visit!"

Determined to explode the myth that women cannot handle money,

Elizabeth proudly reveals what she has learned about the women in her family:

> I had a matriarchal maternal grandmother who ran everything. My grandfather was somewhat docile. On my paternal side, my grandmother was a midwife and earned a bit of money in that manner. Her mother, in England, was a good business woman. She owned row houses which she rented to newlyweds. She also bathed and dressed deceased newborns. Since she knew many grave diggers, she was able to find a place for infants whose parents were impoverished in graves already dug for others. Circa 1880, she traveled alone to the United States at the age of 80, to see her children. She kept her money for the trip in a pocket she made in her petticoat.

Elizabeth went from being a young woman whose brothers were favored over her when it came to choosing an executor for her parents' wills to being the wife of a man who disregarded her knowledge and insisted in 1962 that she sell the beginnings of her first portfolio. In 1964 she recalls quietly opening an account with Prudential and buying one share of IBM. The money came from savings from her household fund. Since she divorced her first husband she has become a financial strategist who not only handles her second husband's accounts but is eager to teach children, grandchildren—anyone who will listen—about the rewards such independence and knowledge bring. "In many ways," she says, "financial freedom is the only path to emotional freedom." I'll close these excerpts by relating one more of Elizabeth's exuberant stories:

> Very often I receive calls asking for my husband. I inquire in what regard, [and it's] often a broker touting the current bond list. I have done all the finances for the past ten to twelve years, and my retort is that this is my responsibility. Most are somewhat surprised. They will usually start out with the obvious, and I love to zap them immediately with quick, knowledgeable questions [about] ratings, call dates, maturity . . . fast, fast, fast. [The broker] will become polite, and maybe even comment that I certainly do understand bonds. What a marvelous feeling I get from these exchanges!
>
> We are not socially active anymore, however occasionally we are in a situation with people in my peer group. If it is appropriate and the economy or the market is mentioned, I usually get

involved immediately. The men become uncomfortable, get quieter, or even wander away. They somehow cannot tolerate women being knowledgeable about something that is traditionally "their field of expertise"!

As I say, Elizabeth is the exception. Irrespective of their class or culture, most women in our society are denied a knowledge of finances, not encouraged to develop the skills they'll need to manage money (theirs or their family's), and are then expected to "take care of business" behind the scenes. We are taught that men need to believe they are in control; and the "good" wife, daughter, sister, secretary, or female co-worker learns to keep things running as unobtrusively as possible; while promoting the fantasy that this or that was the man's idea, resulting from his hard work, is his success. Many women are told they won't *get* a husband or a job if they cannot develop a talent for this pretense.

Who among us hasn't run a household while our husband or father believed the major decisions were his? Or run an office while our boss earned double or triple our salary, receiving the accolades and promotions? We are made to feel that unless we can develop the talents for this subterfuge, and learn to justify our self-effacement and alienation, we will have no future at all. The problem is, in learning the language of oppression we become participants in our own undoing.

In fact, because of their more solid social recognition and greater earning capacity, men generally do hold the power. Women do most of the work with no reward but our intimate knowledge that we are the ones who keep it all afloat. And the language we develop to speak about money makes it more difficult to identify and defeat the forces that oppress us.

It's easy to understand why feminism is reviled when it places women at the center along with men, or—horrors!—simply at the center. Men are viscerally frightened when women demand positions that even *hint* at a reversal or leveling out of the patriarchal power imbalance they have created and traditionally enjoyed. This may explain the exuberant use of such terms as "post-feminist."

But to say that money per se is a negative force is like damning technology because it is so often made to serve profit and mass murder rather than sustenance and healing, greed rather than human need. Neither, however, is money neutral. And women's relationship to it is hardly fixed or set. As we make a solid place for ourselves in the public sphere, that place which for so long was occupied and controlled by men, many of us will necessarily "play the man's game" and attempt to compete on male terms. A proliferation of books and manuals tell us how we can be successful at this. But when women move into previously male-dominated professions, the job categories tend to lose prestige and earning power. It is estimated that when approximately one-third of those employed are women, salaries begin to go down.

Other women, more every day, are developing a different attitude, a different language, a different relationship to money. This comes from our increasingly holistic understanding of how we have been conditioned, manipulated, used, and abused in the various areas of our lives. It is one result of our passionate retrieval of memory and our collective refusal to continue to be set up in all the traditional ways. We are beginning to earn, acquire, spend, invest, share, and think about what money means to us from a female, if not always feminist, consciousness. We are examining the implications of having or not having money, coming to understand some of the traumas its discriminatory handling produced in our own early lives, and learning to avoid repeating these patterns with those we love.

So there's the ongoing effort to obtain legal protection and equal pay for equal work, to get more women into public office, to ensure that we will be able to participate in the decisions that affect our lives and achieve equality in such areas as medical research and insurance. We make progress, suffer setbacks, mobilize, and continue, erratically, to move ahead. But there is also a deeper, more emotionally compelling side of this movement. The rapidly growing recovery community is only one part of the phenomenon. There have been and will be others—from the first small consciousness-raising groups of the early seventies to ecofeminism and the fact that most of our truly great artists and writers are women (many of them women of color).

We are speaking a different language, one that is assertive rather than passive, that calls things by their names, that assigns responsibility. Through a process of coming together, sharing our stories, identifying hidden social patterns rather than isolated individual problems, and revising therapeutic disciplines, we are moving, fast, to a different public as well as private space. We are also beginning to discard the false divisions between these two previously very separate arenas.

As we gain a more complete vision of the healing we need—mind and body as one, not as two unrelated spheres—we see our body politic in new ways as well and are able to speak about it differently. For too long the forces against us have successfully kept us divided; the more spiritual among us willing only to entertain a series of esoteric notions, the pragmatists scoffing at all but a continuation of traditional western male thought (unexamined Plato, Hegel, Marx, Freud). On both sides, a female willingness to honor experience is pushing us to look at and consider the other's contributions.

Today women are effectively shifting a millennial burden of blame from ourselves to our perpetrators and their systems. And with the loss of blame goes a loss of guilt and shame. Such movement, such women's work, profoundly affects how we relate to money. Eventually it must also affect how we speak its name. Nevertheless, in our quest for healthy relationships, we are up against a powerful opponent. Long-held societal norms and mores continue to challenge us, and our progress is not without frustration. In the following chapter we will see how popular culture is used to protect the painful conditioning that has developed around the meaning and value with which we've imbued our monetary exchange.

The Almighty Dollar   **2**
or The Popular Culture of Money

While the poor donned plastic outerware and cardboard
coverings, the affluent ran nearly naked through the
streets, working off power meals of goat cheese, walnut
oil, and crème fraîche.
— Barbara Ehrenreich

Economic systems are not value-free columns of numbers
based on rules of reason, but ways of expressing what
varying societies believe is important.
— Gloria Steinem

Most contemporary societies deify money in one way or another, and
none more than our own. United States popular culture reflects a broad
range of money messages, most of them mixed. These are implicit in
everything from our spiritual practices to the values we assign our
emotional and material exchanges. They can be found in commercial
images, mass media bias, songs and sayings, prevailing attitudes, expectations, and jokes, and are based upon a reverence which is widespread
even when not readily admitted. In our country "the almighty dollar" is
an exclamation that transcends class and cultural lines. All denominations of our coin and paper currency bear the phrase "In God We Trust."[1]

Expressions of irony or scorn also point up the ways in which we hold
a subterranean understanding of the fact that even places of worship are
often ostentatious repositories of wealth, while bank vaults may be
symbolic of our deepest faith. The architect Frank Lloyd Wright, angered
by the refusal of several banks to fund his projects, built at least two of
them in the midwest—resembling churches.[2]

Money and God, if not synonymous, cohabit in a complicated, one might almost say incestuous, relationship. In *The Secret Life of Money*, economist Tad Crawford explains why he believes "money feels to us like language, a great invention whose date of origin is lost in prehistory."[3] In all cultures the tangible objects of exchange have evolved from that which was either nourishing or beautiful: grain, cattle, tobacco, stones, the teeth of dogs and porpoises, strings of cowrie shells, wampum, or the feathers of exotic birds. Crawford makes the leap of defining money as "simply energy . . . the potential for action."[4] But he does not explore its masculinization.

Michael Linton, the founder of a community money system in British Columbia,[5] writes that

> money is really just an immaterial measure, like an inch, or a gallon, or a pound or degree. While there is certainly a limit on real resourses—only so many tons of wheat, only so many feet of material, only so many hours in the day—there need never be a shortage of measure. (No, you can't use any inches today, there aren't any around, they are all being used somewhere else.) Yet this is precisely the situation in which we persist regarding money. Money is, for the most part, merely a symbol, accepted to be valuable generally throughout the society that uses it. Why should we ever be short of symbols to keep account of how we serve one another?[6]

Linton sees money as symbolic of infinite plenitude and as a measure of service rather than of profit or greed. His observation links the care ethic with the meaning of money, clearing the way towards a politics of meaning. Its role in providing for society's disenfranchised is a tragically forgotten aspect of money management about which I will speak in greater detail later in this book.

Jane Jacobs, economist and author of *Cities and the Wealth of Nations*, also sees a region's economy as a living entity, with a language of its own, indeed its own volatile nature: "Currencies are powerful carriers of feedback information and potent triggers of adjustments," she says, "but on their own terms."[7]

James Buchan, journalist and author of "The Psychology of Money," claims that money "is our greatest invention, [that it] has done more to make our civilization even than letters—for these must be translated, whereas money is the language that every human being speaks and understands." And he extrapolates:

> Money has made easy the movements of people and ideas, given us world wars and monuments of architecture, transformed our notions of luxury or want. As a means [it is] almost absolute: it realize[s] every fantasy of creation or murder . . . [can] even give life, in the sense that hundreds of millions of people would not be alive today—could not be fed—but for the pattern of world trade made possible by money . . . at this moment of extreme abstraction, it [is] transforming once again: into an absolute end. Money [is] valued not for its power to fulfill wishes: rather it [is] the goal of all wishes. Money [is] enthroned as the god of our times.[8]

Yes, in our contemporary social confusion, money has become the god of our times. But Linton's and Jacobs's understanding of money as symbolic language remains utopian in our society and Buchan's absolutism and extreme abstraction conflate more than they explain. What more overarching analyses, at a time when specific and palpable crises of all kinds assault us in rapid succession. Buchan's contextualization seems to me the epitome of male definition. How did humankind get from our collective memory of an equitable fulfillment to today's alienating distance and rationalization?

In mythology, money—like so many ideas and processes—actually has a female origin. Money's name, Crawford tells us, derives from the Roman goddess Moneta. Juno, the mother goddess of Rome, stood for fertility and abundance. She was the protector of women, presiding over marriage and childbirth. A multiple deity, Moneta was the name Juno embodied in her role as money's mother. To fully understand the archetypal significance, we must imagine riches, plenty, abundance. Almost all cultures have such fertility goddesses: the Phoenician Ba'al, the Aztec Chicomecohuatl, the Hopi Corn Mother—to name only three.

But we make an even more interesting connection when we move more deeply into the origins of the word; Crawford tells us "the Latin *moneta* derives from the Indo-European root *men-*, which means to use one's mind or think." Thus, "the goddess Moneta is modelled on Mnemosyne, the Greek goddess of memory." In these times of programmed fragmentation, memory can facilitate a necessary reconnection—with our communities and ourselves.

"Contained in the power to remember is the ability to warn, so Moneta is also considered to be a goddess who can give warnings."[9] As we ponder daily monetary exchange and what it means in our lives, we might ask ourselves: warned by whom? and about what? By answering these questions we may reap some valuable clues to money's earliest social role.

As with so many of our long-lost stories, centuries of patriarchal distortion have succeeded in twisting archetypes of harmony and creativity into symbols of power and greed. Women, especially, have been robbed of memory—and the conditions propitious to our developing as independent thinkers. This is why women today demand the right to independent thought, and why the retrieval of memory—both personal and collective—has become such an important step in feminist healing.

The essence of monetary exchange, as it is manifest throughout our history, speaks of a much deeper meaning; one that quite intentionally has been shifted from the female or egalitarian to the male sphere. This shift is most evident in the influence of relatively recent western philosophical thought. Christian mythology describes Jesus expelling the money changers from the temple. Our Judeo-Christian culture has raised a series of barricades, cruel facades around its worship of money.

Nowhere in our mythological history is this linking of money with power more pregnant with the cast of evil than in the image of Moloch, god of avarice and unchecked lust for material wealth. In Allen Ginsberg's poem *Howl*, Moloch has become a seductive and all-powerful being, a metaphor for everything horrendous about modern society—a civilization which has gone mad devouring a people's humanity: "Moloch whose blood is running money! . . . Moloch whose poverty is the specter of genius! . . . skeleton treasures! . . . They broke their backs lifting Moloch to Heaven!" These are only a few of the lines from Ginsberg's litany.[10]

Moloch first came into the Hebrew of the Old Testament from the Greek: Melek, meaning King. After the Captivity and to show their abhorrence of idolatry the Hebrews pronounced it with the vowels of *Bosheth* (shame), establishing a link that continues to this day. Many women, working to reestablish memory in our personal lives, now understand that our first task is to unlearn a particularly debilitating shame.

In Leviticus, Moloch was the name of a Canaanite deity before whom children were burnt and sacrificed in offering. The figure shows up again as one of Milton's devils. And, as our practice of naming follows its discriminatory bent, we find him attached to our uglier species. There is the Moloch Horridus, thorn lizard of Australia, which the Oxford Dictionary describes as "the most grotesque and hideous of existing reptiles." The Brazilian monkey Callitrix Moloch bears the name. And molochize has become a verb: "to imbue with the cruelty characteristic of the worship of Moloch."

So money worship is acknowledged as cruel. But in our Judeo-Christian tradition, money—like the ideal of womanhood—is at once worshipped and despised, virgin and whore, shining coins of flaunted abundance and dirty secret to be hidden or lied about. In contemporary culture, money is proposed as the way to every need fulfillment and simultaneously as a symbol of all that is evil or unclean. One of my respondents quoted a friend who says that "money in this society is treated as shit. No one wants to touch it, see it, or talk about it. Little wonder that paychecks are handed out in sealed envelopes."

The question, however, remains. Does money itself have *anima*, soul? We might begin by asking how soul or spirit is socially constructed in our society, and to what end? Can the giving and taking of money, the process by which it changes hands, be said to *possess soul*, that is, have a spiritual identity, offer spiritual benefits, exert some sort of spiritual power, produce a spiritual revenue?

Since the powerful must develop ideologies to rationalize the exploitation of their victims, they have fabricated stories that link poverty with purity, even godliness. These feature mythological figures or real categories of persons whose purity derives, at least in part, from the fact that they keep no material possessions: Christ, the Catholic saints, Buddhist monks, religious sisters, the starving artist, the innocent hobo, the romanticized homeless person, or any version of a woman who sacrifices her life in service to others.

Until fairly recently, all of these figures were held as exemplary models, to be emulated for virtue's sake. By paying tribute to or helping to support these representations of "the best in us," we may be setting examples that seem attractive in the short term. But we are making three emotional concessions: assuaging whatever obstacle our conscience stumbles upon, justifying ourselves as good by imitation, and excusing or forgiving those who exploit us. All are dangerous aspects of female socialization.

Popular culture has made this a moot point, however, for current social mores no longer really revere or pay homage to such ideals. The prototype who would give up her or his worldly possessions in search of selflessness or generosity is today considered a chump. As the twentieth century stumbles to its anguished close, poverty in the abstract may still equate with purity. But in the concrete reality of life as it's lived—and particularly with the current influence of fundamentalist doctrine— poverty is considered just punishment for laziness, stupidity, addiction— a general worthlessness. Today's poor are hated for being poor. And women—the welfare mother, the "bag lady," the teenage girl who has become pregnant—are vilified with a special vehemence.

Within our more orthodox religious structures, priests and nuns take vows of poverty. They are protected by the patriarchal institution of the Church, and live from its grace. In practice, we can easily see how this ideal of poverty controls the lives of the women (secular as well as religious sisters), while the men (priests, bishops, cardinals, the Pope) enjoy lives of obvious opulence. Today a considerable number of Catholic sisters are leaving congregations they've been part of for years. After lifetimes of devoted service with meager stipends and without benefits, one of the issues that confronts them is the struggle for financial settlements that include some measure of economic security.

As we continue to look at our religious practices, we see that most contemporary experiences of faith include some sort of money giving, a tithe that represents an established percentage of the giver's income. Customarily some, but never all, of this money goes to helping those "less fortunate." Missionary work is vast and varied in purpose: ranging from a very few instances of material aid offered with respect for the recipients to conversion practices that are colonialist at best. Can the latter really be said to produce a spiritual revenue? And if so, does the asset accrue to recipient or giver?

Charitable donation itself is a tricky business. It is not surprising that in our system it gets written off as tax deductible. Certainly there are those who derive a genuine joy in the giving. But society's complex weave of guilt, shame, and sublimation frequently distorts the act. And who but women in our society bear most solidly that burden of guilt, shame, and sublimation?

Our dominant culture has not been very successful at keeping giving free from uncomfortable undercurrents. The spontaneous, genuine, or spiritual sentiments get lost among the more spurious. Money, insofar as it is worshipped in so many of our overlapping cultures, is clearly synonymous with God, despite the chorus of denials this assertion is sure to bring. Consumerism itself becomes a religion, the stock quote or credit card its book of common prayer. And women too often remain the handmaidens of orthodoxy, prevented from equal access or participation while kept busy with the menial service tasks.

A commonly accepted way of defining those beings/things which can be said to possess spirit or to form a part of some larger spiritual whole is whether or not they are recognizably alive. "If it has a face, I won't eat it" is the way one friend has chosen to draw the line. Humans, animals, trees, plants, bodies of water, the air we breathe, the earth itself: all are part of the life cycle. Depending upon our philosophy, we may regard the relationship differently; choosing to wear or not wear animal skins, eat or not eat a variety of dependent species, use only that which is biodegradable, recycle fabricated and natural goods, refrain from polluting the atmosphere.

In many parts of the world, people who live in harmony with the earth speak to what it produces, asking permission to hunt or pluck, talking to plants before removing their medicinal leaves or flowers, exercising a respect and reverence all but lost in this "civilized" time. Establishing such a relationship with plants acknowledges that they hold a life- or god-force. Today there are those who see the advent of agriculture as the single most spiritually injurious moment in human evolution because it forever disrupted this holistic relationship and sent humankind on a downhill spiral with hunger and alienation as its destination.

A relationship with the natural world such as that described above might be said by some to leave money out. But our popular culture swings the pendulum too far in the opposite direction, especially when we consider how money evokes and generates power. To speak of Moloch as the God of Money, to bless a bank note or describe the dollar as Almighty, to clap one's hands and shout "Come on: Big money! Big money!" as the Wheel of Fortune turns,[11] all reflect such tacit acknowledgement.

Perhaps without understanding it completely, we are calling upon Moneta's power, believing in her ability to create abundance and fulfill our needs. Today's acquisition, collection, earmarking, and spending of money may seem quite removed from the practices which denote a reverence for the natural world and its bounty. Yet barter and the use of community currency resurface today throughout our land. If we understand exchange as value ridden (and value producing), our questions about money's spiritual essence become clearer.

Is money also synonymous with love? Popular culture holds some clues, and the commercial advertising to which we are subjected at bombardment levels strongly suggests that it is. The cruise or new car you are urged to buy for an adult loved-one, even the toys you purchase for your children—encouraging them to understand, from an early age, that love is represented by commodities: often the more expensive the purchase the greater the love—are all either overtly or covertly marketed in this way.

The most obvious example is the diamond. From the worthless chip to the many-karat stone, when we set one in a gold band, middle America translates it into commitment. And the equation doesn't stop with engagement. "Tell her you love her all over again" or "Show her you love her as much today as you did then" are phrases from the discourse which accompanies a TV commercial for rings sold to mark ten or twenty-five years of marriage.[12]

I wanted to know if women link money with love, and if so, how the connection is most likely to surface in their lives. On my questionnaire I asked: "Is it easy for you to deal with money within your primary relationship, or relationships you have had? Do you tend to keep finances entirely separate? Somewhat separate? Not at all separate? Have you experienced a financial imbalance between yourself and a spouse or partner? If so, how did/does it manifest itself? How have you dealt with this? Are money and love ever synonymous?"

I received a variety of replies:

"Are you kidding? Well, I'm not sure. . . ."

"If you don't have it, it can be."

"No, of course not, but then again, I like it when my husband surprises me with things."

"I must be independent. If my partner threatens that, it threatens our relationship."

"Even with the money I earned, I was always asking permission and satisfying my mate's needs first. Nothing was ever discussed, and I [feared] that discussion might lead to tension. I [tended to leave] the security of my future to chance and trust that I'd somehow be taken care of. When I understood, in my last relationship which lasted over twenty years, that my mate was more interested in protecting himself from me than in protecting me, I literally became ill. I also lost all sexual desire towards him."

"Money and relationships! Interesting question. I have always kept finances completely separate. . . . I guess this is where my control issues emerge. I don't think that money and love are ever synonymous, but I think my husband does to a degree."

"I have never respected women who stayed in bad or no-longer fulfilling relationships because of economics, but lately I have become a lot more sensitive to this issue."

"My partner earns three times what I do. We keep a joint account by percentage of our income; the rest is ours alone. Money and love are not synonymous in this relationship, but being offered a one-half share in a home I can't afford was to me a very loving act."

"In relationships, the issue of money is a tough one. I tend to buy things for people I care about. This can create an unequal dynamic in which there is an awful lot of resentment and anger."

"Since my money came from my family, it has always been kept in my name. There was a tremendous financial imbalance between my husband and me that added much tension to our relationship. I felt he wasn't even trying to do his share. We eventually divorced, but probably would have anyway. I am concerned and anxious about how to deal with this in future relationships. I should certainly hope that money and love are not synonymous!"

"When we were first married, I was charmed by the notion of a joint account. I think I got a sexual thrill from thinking of merged money. This charm decayed slowly under the pressure of my husband's alcoholism. He never balanced his checkbook and had a childish, magical attitude toward money. Eventually I took over our household finances, although we both were pretty irresponsible. We now keep separate checking accounts and joint savings—and are . . . in Twelve Step recovery programs."

"Money and love have never been synonymous for me, and only somewhat for my mate. It has been difficult though, for us to trust the other. In the past he has often felt left out, superfluous, and like I own everything and he nothing. In the very early stages of our relationship he even worked for me. It has been a long journey for me to learn to let go of power and control, and to build compassion and fair play as the basis of our relationship. I have known, almost from the beginning, that he was not after my money, but my own fears and the tyrannical ways I learned from my family took many years to expunge. I have had to learn to be more generous, to share, to always reach for that which is fair between us. When I asked him what changes he felt he has had to make, he said to acknowledge the weight, responsibility, and complexity of having a large sum of money. He also indicated that he feels his acceptance of this responsibility is an expression of his love for me. Today, having been disinherited, the real difference between us is not that great."

A working-class lesbian wrote: "Are money and love ever synonymous? My aunt (my mother's sister and polar opposite) always said it's just as easy to marry a rich man as a poor one. I'm not interested in either."

All these responses reflect and reedit the memories of money attitudes that shape our earliest years. They acknowledge the ways in which this experience is literally carved into our psyches. They also speak of how money is addressed in popular culture, through our mores, the media, and other socializing influences. A feeling of financial worth or impoverishment affects how we see ourselves, how we react to stimuli from others, how we deal with the issues when we are the ones in control. But there are other important stories, often more difficult to reach.

For example, our collective unconscious holds the painful knowledge that our history includes the buying and selling of human beings. For decades, Africans kidnapped and taken from their homelands were displayed as slaves at auctions and markets in this country; wives and husbands separated from one another, children separated from parents, women robbed of their bodies as well as of their labor. All of them sold.

Poor white women, victims of a less terrible yet also humiliating system, came here as indentured servants. Putting a price on a person imbues that price with hideous meaning, even as it dehumanizes the person for sale and—in less obvious ways—those profiting from or involved in the selling. And this buying and selling of whole groups of peoples foreshadowed a particular denigration for women.

Those of us not directly affected have been conditioned to forget this history, to erase all acknowledgement in our day-to-day activity. The memory, if not explicit, is nonetheless present. When we attempt to understand the power of money exchange, it is an essential as well as horrifying piece of what we must retrieve. Understanding this, it is not surprising that women "willingly," even eagerly, sell themselves in marriage, trading freedom for security, and often rationalizing abuse because it may include what passes for protection.

With the masculinization of our culture, we have lost the stories that tell us who we are. Our civilization has nurtured a Euro- and androcentric vision, one that fears and denies female power, thus burying it or deforming its meaning and keeping us all from healthy equilibrium (for men are also damaged as a result of the oppressive role they are conditioned to play). And we continue to devise and protect systems that avoid the revealing connections. The further we move from our history, the less likely we are to recognize what is at stake. Dominant popular culture has, as one of its several tasks, the perpetuation of memory blackout.

And this blackout has its aids. Modern mechanisms of money exchange—such as credit and debit cards, computer transactions, even to some extent the writing of a personal check—remove the immediacy of barter or of actual coins and bills passing from one hand to another. This makes it easier for us to internalize a fictitious sense of our relationship to our own money, and how we share it with others. We accept the shame and guilt. We allow ourselves to be manipulated, and use money to manipulate others. We convince ourselves that we have enough when we do not, that we can afford something we can't, that we are poor when we have plenty, or that all will somehow work out by the time we are called to accountability.

This contrived invisibility and distance have spawned a relatively new group of industries and professionals: credit card companies, brokerages, financial advisors, financial managers, and financial counselors who work the "magic" of simplifying debt by combining it into a single payment, complete with additional interest and fees for services rendered. Women are conditioned to believe we cannot make our own financial decisions, that we need these experts, and that we ourselves are not likely to be expert material.

The very use of the word plastic to denote the credit card evokes a flimsier or more expendable substance, supporting a sense of lesser worth. Gold is considered the ultimate standard, against which all else is measured. At one time land, crops, animals, even wives represented basic exchangeable wealth. By comparison, plastic struggles to take itself seriously. But this contradiction is no longer productive in today's world of electronic transfers, so further modifications are introduced.

"Take another look at plastic" has become the rallying call of the U.S. plastics industry, which over the past several years has been running a series of TV commercials urging us to acknowledge that goods made of plastic are more than what they seem. These commercials include a variety of items made from the compound, but I would argue that there are other layers of meaning (as there are in all advertising discourse). The inclusion of artificial limbs, knee replacements, and heart valves projects the message that plastic itself is life-giving. "Plastics make it possible" is the final phrase that flashes across the small screen and into our collective consciousness.

Money flow is guided by complex scientific law. It is interesting that physicists are now employed by the major Wall Street financial institutions.[13] Theories about the universe are proving useful in predicting the ups and downs of the market. Relatively recent areas of theoretical inquiry, such as chaos theory, are being applied to the fluctuations in money movement. Still, the myths of patriarchy keep a feminist imagination at bay.

In order to more clearly project our society's ideas of that which is acceptable and that which is not, popular discourse refers to money as dirty or clean. Dirty money may be stolen. It may be counterfeit, come from the profits of a drug deal, accrue from ransom or blackmail, or result from some other operation of questionable circumstance. I remember a television interview with an L.A. gang member who said he was careful about the origin of the money he gave to his church; "Can't give dirty money to the Lord" was the way he put it.

But money may also *feel* dirty because of its frightening association with someone who has hurt us, or because the giver attached intolerable strings to the "gift." Although there may be some consensus as to what makes money dirty, it isn't always possible to clean it simply by changing its use. Most people would say clean money is that which has been honestly earned. But here we run into a much more complex set of questions.

There is all that dirty money that has been laundered, that is to say washed "clean" by virtue of running it through a series of foreign bank accounts or computer operations sometimes established solely for the purpose. The rich and powerful (those generally billed as the cleanest) have an access that ordinary citizens do not; hence the large numbers of people convicted and imprisoned for the smaller monetary crimes, while the crimes involving billions most often go unpunished.

Here, too, the situation is thoroughly gendered. The Wall Street magnate who for years worked a multi-billion dollar market scam is almost always male. The face behind the latest Savings and Loan scandal is a man's. In recent years an increasing number of investment bankers have been tried and convicted for mass corruption previously safe from scrutiny, such as sharing insider information or making quick fortunes off the sale of junk bonds. Almost all of them are men. The 1992 Savings and Loan scandal and the failure of a number of banks have shaken middle Americans who, despite periodic crashes, have been taught a blind faith in this country's financial institutions. At the same time, there are proportionately more women than our percentage of the population serving prison time for bounced checks, credit card fraud, and other of the smaller money crimes.

In our society the popular culture of money frequently shapes our lives in dramatic ways. Its effects can go far beyond temporal issues of loyalty, envy, comfort. The rapid expansion of an ownership class provokes schemes by which the greed of the newly rich begins to threaten the absolute control of those traditional members of the club— who then turn on the newcomers, exposing and punishing their crimes to protect their own. In some cases there is political gain in laying bare the high-level theft which was previously overlooked, such as the crackdown on members of Congress who took personal advantage of those services offered by the House of Representatives post office.

Again, it is important to remember that the vast majority of these mega money crimes are orchestrated by men. Women, as in the more personal one-on-one type of misdemeanor, most often play our role by providing the cover or even the money itself; sometimes giving up lifetimes of work and wellbeing to macho schemes that are but overblown examples of the old con artist's game. The maintenance of attitudes of female dependency upon male control would seem to offer women emotional compensation for what in a more equitable society would immediately be recognized as absurd.

Gender inequity is also quite dramatically present when we compare the way society punishes money crimes. Women in this country typically serve many years of prison time for writing a bad check or for perpetrating credit card fraud. Men—among them respected corporate and financial kingpins—are rewarded with short sentences in resort accommodations for orchestrating vast swindles upon hundreds or thousands of people. And as long as the swindlers are making a profit for corporate America they are generally excused. It is only when the company for which they work begins losing money that they are accused and condemned.

What of the salary drawn from honest labor, but which comes to our employer in a less than honest way? If our taxes go to endeavors we oppose, are we then responsible for what the money buys, or destroys? Is what a man spends on a prostitute dirty money? And does it remain dirty when that prostitute spends it to feed her children? If so, what about the money that supports the wife who for economic reasons stays in a marriage and continues to sleep with a husband she does not love? The gendered nature of all these comparisons is clear.

Restitution is another area where we may observe the contradictions between cultural mandates and the deeper workings of the human psyche. After World War II, Germany was forced to issue lifelong stipends to many of those who survived the horrors of Nazi genocide. I'm told that the very word restitution remains all but unspoken within the Holocaust survivor's community. There were those who refused to apply for the money, knowing nothing could give back what had been stolen. Did they consider it dirty money, or in their agony simply wish to avoid association with those who perpetrated such atrocities against them?

I know something about such dilemmas. At the Congress of Third World Intellectuals, held in Havana, Cuba, in 1968, several hundred artists, writers, scientists, and others signed a document in which we said we would not accept grant monies from Ford, Rockefeller, or other institutions linked to U.S. government policy, so long as that policy exploited and oppressed the peoples with whom we identified and wished our work to serve. This decision was not unanimous; a few refused to sign. And over the next decade a number of other progressive intellectuals were seduced into separating themselves from the declaration, justifying their decisions with the assertion that taking the money and using it against the values of the giver was in itself an act of rebellion.

Similarly, in the 1970's some feminists became quite vocal when the Playboy Foundation offered to fund women's projects; accepting money from the very symbol of female objectification seemed nothing less than a sell-out. Others argued that taking the money created an interesting situation in which they might use it to propagandize the ideas that most profoundly undermine the Playboy system of values. More recently there has been heated disagreement around the monies women have sometimes been able to get from fathers or others who they now remember abused them years before. Within the context of feminist work around incest, some survivors have managed to successfully sue their perpetrators, often to pay for therapy but occasionally also for years of hardship endured. Others, when presented with the option, have preferred to stay away from this source of retribution, dirty in their sense of it, or, again, perhaps too close to the pain.

When there is a charge for healing—which should be accessible to all—an imbalance always results. Later in this book I will talk about sliding scales and other systems that women's communities especially have developed to address the problem of some having more than others. Doctors, therapists, and related health providers wield more than professionalism when they charge high rates for their services; an inequality of power accrues as well. An interesting contrast can be seen between certain practitioners of New Age healing techniques who reap enormous profit and authentic Indian spiritual leaders who will not charge for sweat lodges because, in their world view, healing is not something from which one may make money.

When and how does clean money become dirty? And is it the money itself that is tainted or free of taint, or the way it is used—the process? Some of us would say it is the process. Money itself is only what it buys.

Most of us speak out of one conviction or another in the way we spend our surplus holdings. If we feel very strongly about peace, we may refuse to pay taxes, or that very high percentage of our taxes we know will be used for war. If we invest, we may prefer to put our money into socially responsible mutual funds, and the definition of what constitutes social responsibility also varies. Even the least vehement among us give to causes we believe in, withholding our support from those in which we do not.

For some, buying flowers or a box of candy on Mother's Day signals remembrance and love; others consider such observance a consumerist trap. Costly funerals denote caring to many, excess or waste to others. There are those among us who have been conditioned to measure what they believe they mean to the giver by the size or cost of a gift. Some give only to people who have given to them, and in such cases try to make sure that the gifts are similar in kind and cost. Others prefer to give only what they themselves create, circumventing consumerism insofar as this is possible in our culture. Financial advisors will tell you that as a general rule the wealthy tend towards conservatism when it comes to sharing what they have, while people with much less are often more generous about making contributions to causes and people they believe in.

One issue is how our personal interaction with money may be positively or negatively construed. But a central question continues to be, does any of this use or misuse imbue the money itself with meaning? Or is money a neutral entity, acquiring such meaning only through the process by which it is handled? And, if this latter is the case, why speak of clean or dirty money? Why do some of the religious among us bless a financial windfall? Why do merchants often consider the first dollar of the day to be prophetic of good fortune to come?

Barbara Ehrenreich makes some interesting connections with brilliant tongue in cheek when she points out that although global capitalism depends on markets, markets depend on moods: specifically the mood of the Boys on the Street.[14] And "what is responsible for the mood of the Boys on the Street?" she asks. Why we are, she responds, "because in free enterprise, [the] individual is paramount." As mood is so rarely linked to men in our culture, this analysis bears examination. The emphasis on individuals who, in our system, have almost no control over what is perpetrated in our names, also tends to create a particularly heavy burden for women; born and bred as we are to take society's ills upon our shoulders.

In one of her insightful commentaries, Ehrenreich offers an evocative picture of our economic system and its popular culture fallout. The picture she paints underscores the contradictory nature of money in our lives, examining personal accountability as well as fiscal responsibility. Under the rubric "What You Can Do to Stabilize World Markets and Guarantee Global Prosperity," Ehrenreich suggests some rules for the patriotic (and possibly worried) U.S. citizen:

> Rule 1: Spend. Now is the time to buy everything you have ever needed or wanted, from a two-dollar porn magazine to a dwarf-shaped hitching post for the front lawn . . . every dollar you spend is a vote of confidence for our free-enterprise economy. Every dollar you spend helps employ someone—in the pornography or lawn-statuary industry or wherever—so that they, too, are enabled to spend—
>
> Except that . . . reckless consumer spending created our scandalous $2.5 trillion level of personal debt, which alarms certain key men in Tokyo and Bonn, who in turn are likely to call the men on Wall Street and say, "Whaddya got going there, fellas, a Third World country?" which will bring gloom to Wall Street and penury to the rest of us. Which brings us to:
>
> Rule 2: Save. Sell all your belongings and put the money into a bank, where it will quickly become available to the Boys on the Street for the purposes of leveraged buyouts, corporate takeovers, and other activities that keep them distracted. If you feel queasy about giving up your furniture to provide a larger kitty for those jumpy fellows on the Street, stuff all your assets into a cookie jar. This will help drive up interest rates and make America a more attractive investment to Bonn. However—
>
> The merest upward flutter of interest rates could savage the bond market and reduce the Boys on the Street to craven terror, so it would probably be better to:
>
> Rule 3: Invest all assets in an export-oriented industry—such as TOW missiles or infant-formula mix. This will shift the balance of trade in our favor and bring cheer to the Boys on the Street. If you have trouble thinking of something that American corporations still know how to produce that someone in the world still might want to buy, remember the pioneering example of pet rocks and the great untapped market of southern Sudan. But be careful not to—
>
> Shift the balance of trade so far in our favor that you upset Toshiba and Mercedes, which means Tokyo and Bonn, so—

If her readers ask why two hundred million people should have to pander to the mood swings of a few thousand addicted gamblers, Ehrenreich reminds us that this is what free enterprise is all about, the "freedom to gamble and freedom to lose. And the great thing—the truly democratic thing about it—is that you don't even have to be a player to lose."

The above was written in 1988. Except for the fact that we've left that $2.5 trillion debt figure far behind, it's as applicable today as it was then. More applicable. Because the obscenely wealthy now own more of our country and the world. The number of billionaires on Forbes magazine's 1986 list was almost twice that of the year before, and it continues to rise. The richest 2% of American families now control more than half of all personal wealth in the economy.[15] Or, to put it succinctly, the rich get richer while the poor starve.

Women's lives are profoundly affected—often destroyed—by the realities of the free market economy and by its popular culture makeover. Because we are discriminated against in the work force and played to as mondo consumers. Because we are socialized into dependency upon men, many of whom are also exploited (the syndrome of the man who is humiliated on his job so he comes home and beats his wife, who in turn screams at the kids, who perceive no option but to kick the dog). Because we are reviled if we are lesbians or choose to remain uncoupled. Because we are considered superfluous and then saddled with the responsibility for our own and our children's survival. Because we are relegated to dependency and disparaged when we are old. Because we are feared and despised if we are in any way different from the sanctified cultural norm. Because we are urged to escape into a dream world where families are portrayed as loving, and thirty-something-year-olds sell products for bladder control.

Thinking about money these several years, I would say that a majority of our overlapping cultures—in their variety, and to varying degrees—inject it with godlike attributes. But the deity has become thoroughly male and omnipotent. Those of our cultures which reject this sort of deification must vie with the dominant one for their survival and a winning strategy is rarely on their side. Witness Native American attempts at reintroducing alternative value systems or the difficulties encountered by small independent businesses, or spiritual, back to the land, or drop-out counter-cultures, when they try to operate by a system of life-affirming values within the capitalist paradigm.

For women, the dilemma is complex. Successive waves of feminism have begun to crack the solid shell of patriarchy; more slivers of light now shine through multiple holes in a once tightly woven fabric. Still, society, with its thoroughly male ownership of power at all the most important levels, produces as many frustrations as it obscures choices. Those who seek relationships of justice often find ourselves bouncing off the walls.

I am reminded of an experience I had during my years in Cuba. The North American man with whom I was then living and I had been struggling for some time with issues of sexism in our relationship. Like so many white, middle-class men of the seventies, he talked a great equality line but balked and found ways to evade his stated beliefs when it came to actually doing his share of housework or childcare. Like so many white, middle-class women of the seventies, I wasn't going to give in or give up. At a particular point in this struggle, we found it possible to agree that if our youngest daughter was sick, whoever had the lesser work load at his or her job that day would stay home and care for her. The other would go to work as usual.

But this decision, a product of such intense personal struggle, broke down in the larger social context. If I stayed home with our baby, no matter what was on my day's work agenda my boss and colleagues were likely to accept the situation. They saw a mother necessarily attending to her sick baby. If my child's father stayed home, the response was quite different. Despite the Cuban revolution's by then considerable advances in gender equality, neither his boss nor coworkers really accepted my partner's choice. What in me was seen as duty became absenteeism when exercised by him.

Women trying to develop a healthier relationship to money often come up against similar barriers of resistance. Systems of change may be struggled for and even obtained, at home or in a circumscribed community, but they tend to break down when challenged by larger social tradition. Indeed, like streaks of light running through the responses to my questionnaire, there are numerous stories of parents attempting to establish healthier money relationships with their children, heterosexual couples trying to handle their finances in less patriarchal ways, and certainly lesbians for whom new ways of looking at money are but one part of the overall creativity necessary to the development of a more functional family dynamic. Alternative lifestyles, options, risks, aren't made easy, though. We may find the old ways of doing things emotionally impoverishing, even oppressive, but when our new ideas meet the hard walls of social convention they often shatter at our feet.

The hidden anxiety, fear, shame, guilt, defensiveness, and even rage that arise when money is the subject of conversation or debate are nowhere more explicit than in a game played by members of the old At The Foot of the Mountain, a women's theater group active in Minneapolis throughout the 1980s. Plays often emerged from collective discussion on a particular theme. Martha Boesing, who was the group's director, says they had always planned to stage a production on the theme of money, "but it was one of those plays we never got around to, perhaps partially out of fear." Then she shares the group's experience when one night, as a prelude to discussing the writing of such a play, the women sat in a circle to play a money game.

Each woman was asked to put all the money she happened to have on her at the time in a pile in front of where she was sitting. A leader started with instructions like "Give all your money away to anybody or anybodies in the group." Or "Tell your neighbor what you think she should do with her pile of money." Or "Decide collectively who in the group needs the most money, and why. Then set up a fund for her with everyone contributing a percentage of their pile." The suggestions continued; readers might add some of their own.

Martha says more tension arose that night than she'd seen in the history of the group. Finally, the woman leading the game instructed everyone to put her money in the center of the circle. When they'd complied, she told them to take back only what they thought they deserved (here the word *need* may be substituted for *deserve*). When everyone had done this, she told them, simply, "Okay, that's your money. Game's over."

Many of the women were furious. They had never doubted that they would have the opportunity to get back at least what they'd put in— perhaps more. Because of the complicated symbolic value money holds in our lives, those playing the game felt coerced, tricked, betrayed. They were unable to relate in a positive way to what this shared experience told them.

So, does money have soul?

Of course it does.

Soul is as soul does. We may use different words to describe that essence which lifts a being—person, animal, plant, even an idea or object we imbue with a life of its own—to a category that reverberates within, capable of changing us. For many it will constitute heresy to give money such stature. Few, however, will deny that we inhabit a relationship with money that holds us in a similar powerful grip, pushing us to our most ruthless and then pulling us back to our most generous self, often alternately and without warning.

It is in our recognition of money as process rather than as immutable thing, lifeless and unchanging, that we may understand its spiritual and most powerful dimension and may find our way to its retrieval. In the following chapters we will hear from women struggling with the issue of money in their lives, and from some who—in the family or larger community—are evolving innovative alternatives to its traditional misuse and manipulation.

Mint Condition(ing)   3
or The Generational Curse

I have peeled away your anger
down to its core of love
and look mother
I am   a dark temple
where your true spirit rises
 . . . I learned from you
to define myself
through your denials.

—Audre Lorde

I wish I could dig up the earth to plant apples / pears or
peaches on a lazy dandelion lawn / I am tired from this
digging up of human bodies / no one loved enough to
save from death

—June Jordan

Family—traditional, alternative, functional or dysfunctional—is the
smallest human group within our social organization. As such it is
unique, while mirroring the forces that exist in the larger configuration:
relationships in which one person is generally in control and another—or
others—is controlled.

In our society a family may consist of a father, mother, and children.
Perhaps there are no children; still, the couple is a family. Especially
among American Indians, African Americans, and those who have
recently immigrated, extended arrangements are common; grandparents,
uncles and aunts, cousins, and others may be included. A teenage mother
and her child are a family. A lesbian couple with children form a family

in which there are two mothers. Gay men make families. Friends who come together around shared ideals design alternative families. Heterosexual women—through divorce, widowhood, abandonment, or choice—may also find themselves at the heads of families in which there are no men.

But in patriarchy, male power is always present; if not in the person of an individual man then through the social norms men establish, the kinds of relationships they exalt, and the power they wield. Depending upon the family, a husband may enforce his decisions by the use of violence or a woman who has been hurt in her family of origin may seek refuge in behavior designed to keep some measure of control while enabling the man in her life to believe he is in charge. Women and men may discuss important issues and come to agreement together, sometimes even with their children when these are old enough. Coded words and gestures—an intimate language—permeates each type of relationship, shaping and protecting its reproduction in those coming up. The more devious the imbalance, the more dependent upon a complex set of myths.

Families evolve their own mythology, born in the histories of their primary members. But these myths are not played out upon a neutral stage. Conflicting interests tend to direct the family drama, and money often becomes one of its most readily accessible props. Attitudes around the inhibition or freedom with which money is exchanged, the manipulation or abuse attached, define that practice accepted as normal within a family. Members are accustomed to the script; they know who directs, who the star is, and the penalty for ignoring stage directions. Outsiders may not have a clue.

Women who as children were taught they "cost" too much may buy unneeded items randomly in adulthood, or develop a frugality unrelated to their means. Or they may pretend hardship, creating a myth of poverty and talking constantly about bargains while secretly indulging themselves. In their discourse the myth takes over. The messages they emit are confusing to say the least. The contradictions between myth and reality may repeat themselves for generations to come, descendants not even really understanding why they hold the attitudes they do. As those who inherit the distortions reach the age of accountability, this contradictory behavior has moved further from its source but is also more set: a solid dysfunctionality.

One woman may have a great deal of money yet call herself poor. Another may be struggling but describe herself as "middle class" —that particularly North American category that is often more aspiration than definition. One who can barely afford to lend money to a friend may do so without giving it a second thought. The loan returned may even elicit surprise. Another may succumb to the pressure of such a request, then wonder every day when it will be repaid. Neither of these attitudes may have anything to do with how much money the lender has; most often it will have been shaped by family mythology.

Poverty functions as reality and as myth. Jeannette, in her late forties, comes from a white working-class family and a childhood that engendered complex ambivalence about money. She is married to a man whose background is slightly more comfortable; he helped raise her son and daughter from a previous marriage and now also supports her full-time attempt to generate her share of their income from writing. Jeannette speaks first of her childhood:

> We lived, like most working-class people, from paycheck to paycheck. There wasn't a lot of money . . . but we weren't desperately poor either. I remember clearly my mother's saying, "We're poor people," and recognizing that as an exaggeration. My Dad said that during the war he had seen children in Europe eating out of garbage cans. Now *that* was poor. . . .

Jeannette and her family lived in trailer homes. She hated that, but more because of its nomadic aspect than because the trailer wasn't nice enough. "I wanted to stay put," she says, "like other people."

> My grandmother lived in Grand Junction, Colorado, in a small house that was magical to me because it was *her* house. . . . Now I realize that it was very humble, three rooms plus a bathroom so small that you had to sit sideways on the toilet; it fit the room wall-to-wall, and you had to step over it to get to the shower. There was no tub. The refrigerator was on the screened-in front porch. I suppose the house was 500 to 600 square feet. I knew she lived on a pension of $106 a month.

A sense of place, a place of her own, was what Jeannette grew up wanting most. Her grandmother's tiny home was precious, because it was *hers.* The trailers meant transience, impermanence. Today a modest home with enough land for her horses and other animals is central to her sense of security, well-being. The fear of being placeless can be linked to a lack of control. And as a child she never felt in control of even the occasional cash that came her way.

Jeannette wasn't given an allowance and although she remembers being given small amounts whenever she asked for them, she felt uncomfortable at not being able to count on any sort of regular money— no way to save or plan. Today she admits that she tends to "become very close only to people from roughly the same economic background." Those who grew up with more, especially, make her uncomfortable; they don't seem to read her well, or pick up on the almost automatic cues that guide her responses in human interaction.

The same words or phrases may hold dissimilar meanings in families where they have been differently coded. Take an apparently casual question: "We can't really afford that, can we?" Even for women of equal incomes, the implications vary. For one, the question is verbalized thought, no more or less than what it says: "Can we afford this? I guess not." For another it translates as "I really want this, and would appreciate your buying it for me. But you must protest the implications of my question and then take the initiative." A husband's or partner's failure to respond as expected may provoke disappointment, even anger. In yet another woman the same words signal a wistful statement of fact, not even requiring confirmation. Need, desire, resignation, anticipation: each must be interpreted according to the myths in place.

A woman goes to a restaurant with friends. When the check arrives she divides it among the group, assuming everyone is as willing as she is to split the total. Another seethes silently; in her concept of financial exchange one should not be expected to pay for what one hasn't eaten. Money issues being as difficult as they are for her, she cannot express her discomfort in words. Eventually she may stop eating out with these friends. A third woman would just as gladly have picked up the tab. A fourth is disappointed she did not. These attitudes have nothing to do with what each of these women has in her bank account or carries in her purse. They reflect her money mythology, a set of attitudes traceable to much more than wealth or poverty.

Peculiar little habits of money exchange as well as the more flagrant misuse of money as control move from generation to generation, picking up speed as they go. The baggage becomes heavier, its evidence more of a nonsequitur. For those who have acquired a certain level of understanding, it may also be less acceptable. As with other sorts of abuse, only a coming to consciousness and the decision to break with destructive patterns is capable of exposing the myths.

These surface in so many of my narrators' stories. Often the memory has to do with the need to safeguard masculine pride, and the threat of shame if this is not accomplished. Carla, a working-class respondent to my questionnaire, remembers that her mother handled the family's money but made sure it looked like her husband did: "When we went out to eat—usually at the Harvest House or at the mall—she would hand him some bills under the table so that he could pick up the check." If she examines the behavior and its ramifications, the adult woman with this sort of childhood experience will make sure she doesn't repeat it. The woman unable to look at such patterns most likely will recreate them.

Esther is a Jewish woman in her mid-fifties. Divorced and with a grown daughter, she teaches college math as well as carrying a full agenda of community and other political work. Esther's childhood, not unlike many, included incest and its consequent denial. Her mother, because of her own painful history, was unable to nurture or protect her:

> One of my mother's major strategies for negotiating her life is still "deny and ignore." Her bitterness at what happened to her family (her mother, father, and younger brother were killed in a concentration camp in 1943, when I was two years old) and her inability to grieve the tragedy have taken their toll. She only showed me the last letter from her own mother, and the one from the Red Cross confirming their deaths, within the last five years. She told me she never cried over them, then entered her bedroom for several minutes and came out. This "deny and ignore," and her inability to grieve, diminished the meaning of any other situation for which grieving might have been appropriate. They were accomplices to [my experience of] incest....
>
> Related to the incest is my mother's fear of me. A few years ago, as a throw-away remark, she said "You don't know how afraid I am of you." I now think: of course you are. You are afraid that I will raise the unrelenting horrors of my childhood, in which your neglect played a major role.... This unspoken guilt and the fear of

issues being raised, leads my mother to a tangible paranoia which she places between us.

Finally, something which confuses things further is that she shares some of her material wellbeing with my daughter and me. I ask myself: am I further obligated if I accept her money? I am not at peace with this yet, though I do think I should not have to feel grateful. She is in no way sacrificing any of her own well-being, but it is still a little messy for me.

Just how messy is clear in Esther's following admission:

As a professor of mathematics, people assume I can keep my own checkbook balanced. I cannot. And I had taught mortgages for years when I went to buy my own home; I had the knowledge but couldn't use it. I am sure this was influenced by the relationship between myself and my mother, since the down payment was her money.

In this family, the inability to speak about what happened many years ago perpetuates a pain that is borne in silence. Myths were constructed because they seemed necessary to survival when in reality they obstructed or delayed the possibility of healing. Esther's story holds a dramatic connection between the trauma of the Holocaust and the trauma of her own childhood sexual abuse. Unable to work towards resolution, the victims themselves become abusers. Money handling is but one of the terrains upon which feelings of uncertainty and betrayal continue to reproduce themselves. Esther is beginning to break the silence—and the chain of dis-ease—by looking at the myths.

For another of my narrators, trauma originated in an unexplained event having to do with her father's business. Malka is a psychologist in her fifties, white, mother of two sons, divorced and remarried, comfortable. A sudden change in her childhood economic status, and the accompanying silence and fear, profoundly marked her life and sense of self-worth. She traces serious bouts of depression, an early inability to place herself where she wanted to be, and the failure of her first marriage to this sudden economic shift and the way her parents handled it. This also shaped the ways in which she chose her profession, handled divorce, and manages financial matters with her own children.

Malka's father was a small contract clothing manufacturer in New Jersey, in business with his brother before the mid-century shift in the industry. She describes the first half of her childhood as comfortably middle-class, with the family business doing well. Then an unacknowledged problem between the two patriarchs tore brother from brother, sending the family economy into a sudden downward spiral:

> There was a blow-up . . . friendly relations were severed. I did not see my cousins for thirty years. As I write this I realize how frightening and dramatic [it all] was. Nothing was explained to me. I was left with a sense of badness and shame. Who was bad? Me?

Malka looks back and sees that

> because of my hatred of business I was ripe for the radicalism of the '60s. I felt the need for social justice and for the creation of new societies based on more fair and equitable economic systems. I wanted to live on a kibbutz in Israel where all differences between people based on money and status would be eliminated. I got caught up in the Civil Rights and anti-war movements instead.
>
> And I became profoundly lost when I married and turned over the direction of my life to my [first] husband. It was okay to be poor and to have nothing during the early years of our marriage. We were into the romance of the Movement. But once I had children, the security needs which originated in my family of origin reared their ugly heads and began undermining the marriage and my ideals. I felt I needed to raise my children in a middle-class life style and give them a greater feeling of security than I had had. I didn't want them to be limited by the fear, anxiety, and depression which have limited me.

Malka began pushing her husband to be more upwardly mobile, more successful in his field. In part as a result of the ensuing tension, the marriage began to disintegrate.

> I took a conventional path and became a social worker in one of our society's dominant institutions, the schools, because I knew it was secure and paid the best salaries. This was a betrayal of what was best in me, the daring, creative, and intellectual parts. . . . When my marriage fell apart I was able to keep my home, support my children and get them through college and launched into the world (with the help of their father of course). . . . I have helped many children and families in my work, but my voice is weak and I am basically invis-

ible. I wanted to be a presence but I opted for relative security instead. The depression and anxiety which have plagued me most of my life is likely the result of choosing safety over self-expression.

Hopefully, the understanding Malka has gained of the damage her parents' silence inflicted upon her life and her willingness to talk about it with her sons will help them avoid having to grapple with similar issues. It is a sad commentary on our society that the choices are so often posed this rigidly: security versus creativity, tradition versus initiative, or a capacity for taking risks, responsibility versus happiness.

For women raised to entrust their futures to someone other than themselves, the trap can be even more complex. By the time some of us come to understand that there are options apart from those we've been handed, valuable years have been taken from us—and our creative energy made much more difficult to retrieve.

A shared experience among the women who responded to my questionnaire is that of being kept ignorant of their family's financial situation. This ignorance breeds confusion, and later perhaps also anger. Myths are created to explain what might so easily have been explained by simple truth. Judith, a white working-class narrator in her mid-forties who has returned to school and is trying to professionalize, admits

> to this day my family's financial situation is a matter of considerable controversy and distress. When my parents wrote their wills I realized they had much more money than I previously imagined. This made me feel very angry. I believe that if they had invested this money on a house in a better neighborhood it would have had a positive impact on my life. Because I grew up in a working-class neighborhood, the education I received was much poorer than that of most of my contemporaries in my field.

In some families, keeping money matters secret is simply custom, reflecting the idea that one "doesn't wash one's dirty laundry in public." In such cases ignorance is not necessarily accompanied by confusion, nor does it produce later feelings of anger or betrayal. Perhaps it depends upon how comfortable the parents themselves feel with how they have organized their family life. Kit is a Hawaiian Japanese American in her early forties. A painter and poet, she was trained as a social worker and has gone back to school for an advanced degree in art therapy. Her husband is a psychiatrist. Of her childhood Kit remembers

> I understood that we did not have much money to spend for what were considered luxuries, e.g., butter, whole milk, sodas, ready-made clothes, fashionable shoes, bicycles. We made do with nutritious but less expensive alternatives, clothes that would last, hand-me-downs; would make up games with available "junk." [However] the specific money situation was not discussed with the children. I don't believe my oldest sister knew significantly more than I did about our family financial situation.

More often, though, secrecy points to layers of cover-up and denial. Amanda is a philosopher and dream counsellor in her early fifties, white, twice married and divorced, and with grown children. She later claimed her lesbian identity and now lives with her partner of many years. Amanda comes from an upper middle-class family in which she is the only daughter. She had a brother and a sister. One committed suicide and the other was killed shortly afterwards in an automobile accident. She describes her family of origin as

> very patriarchal . . . Lacking any formal religion, upon reflection I would say that money was the unspoken religion of my youth. It was apparent that there was more than [enough], but that it was somehow unreachable, something to be savored but not used, something, like religion, that required an intermediary.

Amanda goes on to explain that her father handled all financial matters; he was the intermediary in that church, its high priest. "He considered that women were not capable of understanding or making financial decisions." She remembers him "asking Mother to sign the tax return while holding his hand over the figures so that she could not see what she was signing."

When such basic information is kept by a husband from his wife, what else may be hidden? And what is hidden from the children? Patriarchal attitudes of secrecy and unilateral control come to fruition in a woman's developing sense of dependency, low self-esteem, and narrowed possibilities. Amanda emphasizes the fact that money became the main measure of value in her family, and that it was thoroughly gendered:

As a girl I was not supposed to become a professional or to earn money because that was a man's job. . . . My father believed his wealth made me a more valuable commodity. I was to marry someone with money and gain my status by being subsumed into his. . . . All of my aspirations for careers were unsupported and I was sent off to college to find a husband. I definitely used money as a power tool in my marriages. But as it became clearer to my parents that I could [not] and would not follow the expected path, their perception of my relationship to money and to being female became more ambivalent. Now it has reached the place where my mother is always asking me if I am being paid for what I do. My worth is judged by what I make. Does this mean I am no longer a woman?

Amanda has spent many years consciously divesting herself of the attitudes that were such an integral part of her growing up. Divorce, more than one career change, coming out as a lesbian, periods of ill health and severe depression (which she traces to psychic damage) have all been mileposts. She is aware that she passed many of the attitudes foisted upon her on to her own children, with whom she occasionally still has discussions about their disparate expectations. The early images are kept vivid and threatening, since Amanda travels once a month to attend to her parents' affairs. But they are now elderly (her father more vegetative than alive), so the threat is a pale version of its former self.

The way a family handles money symbolizes more than simple exchange. It is a metaphor for power that moves from one generation to another, acquiring new myths along the way. Bernarda is a Mexican American journalist and author in her mid-forties whose father was the first in his family to go to college. During her childhood and youth, her parents attained middle-class economic status.

While Dad brought in the income, Mom's role was to pay the bills, balance the checkbook, etc. She was often frustrated that my father would not participate in the decision-making about budgeting. When she brought it up, he often exploded. He couldn't understand what she was complaining about. After all, the money was there, wasn't it? Well, yes and no, depending on how well you budget, my mother would try and say.

The way finances were handled in Bernarda's family of origin strongly affects her own current struggles; she married a man who is trying to make it as a freelance photographer, and admits to frequently taking out her frustrations in discussions about how much he is able to contribute to their joint economy. She wants to be supportive, but finds old ghosts getting in the way.

A variety of experiences may conspire to provoke certain women to turn against their backgrounds and pursue values disdained by their class or culture of origin. Jane, a Bay Area muralist and graphics designer, was the artist, the "different" one in her comfortable white suburban family. Race and racial privilege were indelible markers as Jane grew up. As is true in so many women's lives, serious illness opened her to a greater understanding of the forces that have shaped her life. Surviving cancer urged her to make changes.

> East Coast Upper Middle Class Suburban [is] a way of describing our family's living outside Washington DC, outside Boston, outside New York, but coming from a particular culture and class which had greater impact on us than the characteristics of the town we lived in.

After many more reminiscences of that upper-middle-class culture, Jane begins to touch on what seemed other:

> Where things felt different was in relation to the black people in our lives. Bertha took the bus in from town along with other people working in Hollin Hills. I became especially aware of economic differences between her family and ours when for one reason or another my mother and I would visit her in her house. Her husband "did not work," and she had "too many children," according to my mother. . . . For many years I took for granted the upbringing with a black maid, then blocked the fact out through the '60s and '70s, embarrassed by the stereotypical inequality. In recent years, remembering, I cherish the association with these real women, eating their food, hearing their language, feeling the care they gave me.

From a family in which the father worked, the mother had given up an early career as a newspaper reporter, and the offspring were expected to attend good colleges and professionalize, Jane broke with that tradition:

> My father was diligent in saving money. My grandmother's money was from "careful investing." I of course resisted all this. . . . I [grew up thinking] money would just happen without careful planning. I was not prepared to run a business or assume long-term financial responsibility for myself. If my family of origin had had less money I [might have] felt more drive to "get ahead."
>
> Because I was the artist in the family, I think everybody wrote me off from having a mind for business or self-reliance. I was to become the educated artistic wife, according to the expectations of my gender and class in those years. [But] I left marriage plans and the beginning of a career at Random House and headed for San Francisco in 1970, with the assumption that I'd find work and a way to live.

The Bennington graduate and talented artist embarked on what were to be many years of trying to survive from her art. She lived collectively, had a child with a man who turned out to be addicted to drugs, became a single mother, and eventually settled in her current relationship. At age 47 she says:

> I've come to rely on a shared income for the first time in my life. [My son's] father had taken money from me. Now there is someone who wholeheartedly embraces [our] life, pays for private school for my son, has contributed to my business set-up, bears the major responsibility for our house.

The relationship provides a different sort of context and important support, but hasn't entirely erased Jane's fear:

> We make decisions regarding money well together. And frequently have discussions with my son about his responsibilities. . . . I now feel an intense desire that my business support me. [But] having become a shared family financially, I get scared something will happen to [my companion].

Jane also recognizes that she has passed her ambivalent approach to money on to her son:

One needs to earn it, but there it is anyway ... being cute and manipulative will get you the things you need.... I felt guilty about no father for him and would overdo birthdays, not teach him "the value of a buck." ... In my experience, the most profound myth about women and money is that women can work and handle money well, but don't have to if a man is around. That the '50s pushed women in my class away from financial responsibility is evident in my family.

Conscious women can be powerful in their ability to look at where they come from, where they're headed, and make whatever adjustments may be necessary in order to change directions, even when this means breaking with long-held custom. Sometimes those from the most apparently traditional families strike out to create the life they need.

Shirley and her identical twin sister Doris grew up in the depression years in a "well-to-do Jewish family" in which their father had a successful real estate business in a poor area of Philadelphia. Their mother and an older brother completed the picture, which was fairly stereotypical: a father who brought money home to a mother who managed the household affairs.

In her own time Shirley would nurture a family that was anything but traditional. She left an unhappy marriage, as she describes it, because her husband "had to make all decisions for all people all the time." Their three grown daughters are lesbians. And Shirley enlarged her family to include adopted daughters and sons from several other cultures. In her seventies today, she continues to work and to be socially and politically active while exuberantly attending to numerous offspring and grandchildren.

Shirley's formative years hold clues to her later decisions. When they were still in high school, the twins' brother shared his college math homework with them and the circumstances of World War II unexpectedly belied the gender roles of the times by recruiting these young women for unusual defense work:

Doris and I were both excellent in math ... most women were interested in the social sciences, history, and education. Men who were qualified to work in math and science were in the service. So we were recruited right out of high school, in June 1942. We had planned to be full-time students at the University of Pennsylvania, but a letter from the War Department came before [our high school] graduation.

That letter opened the door to intensive training and then to jobs in an office where eighty women, recruited from all over the East Coast, worked in three shifts around the clock. They did ballistics research and traced bombing trajectories for U.S. Air Force operations in Europe. Shirley and Doris were the youngest. They worked 48 hours a week and managed to start college in their "spare" time. They earned $12,000 a year, extraordinary pay for women in those days—particularly for such young women.

Shirley and her sister won citations for this work, which was assumed beyond the capabilities of women until the shortage of men made hiring them a necessity. After the war both women married. Then their lives took different turns, although they have always remained close, with that intense identification so many twins share. Shirley married a man who tried to build a business for which she had a much better head than he. This, among many other contradictions, eventually led to their divorce. Doris remained happily married, but was widowed when her husband died in middle age.

Shirley and Doris eventually went into business together. They formed the first woman-owned real estate company in Philadelphia, drawn to the profession partly because it had been their father's, but also because their neighborhood was integrating and they wanted to contribute to that process that was being opposed by so many who feared that the entrance of blacks would lower property values. Shirley, especially, has long been active in social justice work. For both women, opening their own realty company had as much to do with an ethic of justice and caring as it did with its being a business that would enable them to support themselves and their numerous children. Shirley continues:

> In 1960, Doris got a "salesman's license," as they called it in those days, and opened a branch of the business, using our father's name as sponsoring broker. Her husband did the legal work and provided a lot of the funding . . . and a mother's helper came in to take care of the kids so she could go to work.

In order for the business to be in her name instead of our father's, Doris had to take extra credits, pass a test, and become a broker. While preparing for that test, she insisted that I take the sales licensing exam, so I did. In 1961, when I got my license, we went in . . . together. In 1964 I finally took the broker's exam and we changed the name of the office to Twin Realty: the only all-woman's real estate company in the city. We worked together as partners for almost 28 years.

Especially in the forties and fifties, when a male/female two-parent family was the norm, a father's absence was almost invariably the source of insecurity. Economic class was more solidly set then as well, and further conspired to shape a child's feelings. Helga is a university professor of white working-class origin who has struggled against feelings of inferiority all her life, surrounded as she is by colleagues who come from families much richer in material and intellectual possibilities.

Complex issues marked Helga's childhood. Her father disappeared, and for years her mother, unable to cope, placed her and her brother in foster homes. Abandoned by her husband, she in turn abandoned her children. The myths created in order to justify this behavior have taken their toll on Helga's sense of self-worth. She grew up, married, and divorced, and today has a teenage son. They live with her long-time woman companion, who is a lawyer. Recently turned fifty, Helga remembers her childhood as one in which she

> was taught to always appear as if [I] had more money than [I] did, and that associating with those who had less could . . . bring you down to their level in the eyes of others. . . . Poverty meant a great deal of shame and sense of unworthiness. [I was] taught the value of money mostly by the lack of it. I knew nothing about savings or bank accounts until I went to high school and was in bookkeeping and accounting classes. But even then it was for other people, not me.

Helga speaks of her childhood clothing being mended and mended again, and admits to finding it particularly difficult not to immediately sew the holes that appear in her son's. "I cannot force myself to buy for him 'pre-torn' or 'prestained' clothing," she says. "When I grew up, you wore only the best clothes in public. If torn they were neatly patched, if stained they were not worn."

When Helga's son wanted to wear pants that were ripped at the knee, a particularly North American middle-class fashion statement of the young, it was hard for her to deal with what she calls "such over-romanticized pandering to an illusion of the working class." Her son must cope with her views, as well as fit in with other kids at school: "He and I talk endlessly about these conflicts," she says, "and what these clothes mean to him, and to me."

It is interesting that Helga's brother, although he suffered the same childhood privations she did, became an adult who mismanaged and then lost what meager money their mother had acquired. He was the man, and, as such, was given the responsibility of handling the family finances. Helga and her partner now make monthly contributions to her mother's living expenses. The mother, however, remains closer to the son who brought her to the edge of poverty than to the daughter who attends to her survival. This is not an uncommon ending to such stories. Helga herself sees want as having marked her life in positive as well as negative ways.

> Not having all the endless privileges of the middle class [means] I am more independent and self-reliant than most. I don't take financial things for granted. It took me a long time to learn how to do banking and save; I still bounce checks on occasion. [Having been working class] gave me a strong foundation with working people on which to build a theoretical political stance.
>
> I have often "married up" and that creates its own self-hate as well as problems with partners over class issues. [My partner] and I had a hard time in the beginning until she understood how thoroughly I am affected by my class and by hers, and how deeply she acts out of class as do we all. Now we can almost spot a class issue before it hits, but it has taken years of work and struggle.

Generational damage recedes slowly, and only beneath the assault of conscious hard work. Trudy is a nurse in her early fifties, divorced and the mother of two grown children. Money took dramatic turns throughout her life. She was raised in a mansion by parents who had somehow managed to acquire it although they couldn't afford to hire the servants necessary to its care. Both Trudy's mother and father were alcoholics and died in their fifties. Trudy's family income rose and fell. She didn't feel she fit in the neighborhood of her youth. Before her divorce, Trudy's husband became a well-known novelist. She says:

> In my marriage [my husband] made a lot of money and we were hippy-ish so it wasn't particularly an issue except that I felt such a weak identity that my being able to make my own life was immediately important not so much from a money standpoint as from a standpoint of "and what do you *do?*" Now, since we divorced, for twenty years my living has been mine.

This sense of self-ownership is always precarious, though. Trudy took an early retirement in order to have more time for long dreamed-of pleasures. Yet she continues to work fifty- and sixty-hour weeks, patching together the job opportunities that provide the income which keeps her living hers. In her current relationship she continues to live in her own home while her partner lives in his; she may be wary of merging the independence that was won through so much struggle.

When female ancestors held power, a family's history will reflect that. Poverty and other hardships may be present, myths may be fabricated as cover-up or to ease the pain. But that female strength passes from one generation to the next, keeping faith with the future. Joy is a Creek Indian woman in her mid-forties. She married young, as her mother had before her, and had a son and a daughter in successive unions. Now she is a well-known poet, musician, and university professor—a grandmother who shares her life with her partner, who is a lawyer. Her daughter, son-in-law, and granddaughter periodically stay with them. The class, culture, and attitudes around gender that were a part of Joy's youth can be seen—and felt—in her current attitudes.

> In my father's family the women were the power: my grandmother and aunt were born into wealth, got BFAs in art, handled money. My aunt had a jewelry shop . . . painted and lived on her own. My grandmother died when my father was young, but she handled the money in her life, though her husband stole most of it after her death. The Creeks were matrilineal and the culture had an inherent respect for women. Of course Christianity changed some of the form.

As in many families, class was complicated by race. Indian women, forced to deal with men who are also oppressed by the dominant society, develop a strength that lives in Joy's bones. In her story, class imploded, somersaulted, and experienced dramatic change. She remembers that her mother's parents lived in a one-room, later a two-room house, and had no electricity or running water. But her father

> was born in a 21 room house. His family were rich Creeks. In the neighborhood in which we lived before the divorce, the families were mixed Indian and white, all of a similar lower middle-class status. I wasn't aware of economic differences, except through stories of what had been lost in my father's family. After the divorce and my mother's remarriage I was constantly aware of the struggle to put food on the table, and often felt guilty for eating.

Here money came to equal worth and status. And race and money were grafted one upon the other in ways that are not easily decipherable:

> I was taught that my relatives who had less, my mother's family of brothers and their wives, were lazy and ignorant. I felt a distinct disregard by these relatives for a brother whose wife was Mexican. This aunt and uncle followed the harvests some years in the summer and had four children. They were never dressed as well as my mother's attempts to dress us, at least that was my perception then. But there's more history here. This brother terribly abused my mother. And though my mother is Cherokee and her brothers mostly married full-blood Cherokees, and she married a Creek man, there was a lot of internal racism. Race meant less money to her, though the man she married came from a wealthy Indian family.

When her father left and her mother remarried, Joy began to know real poverty—its stigma and pain:

> I knew the money came from my mother's body, could see the toll exacted in varicose veins, a burn from a frylator machine that ran up her arm, her exhaustion. So I did what I could to relieve her by giving her a bath, polishing her work shoes, and ironing her clothes. I babysat, sold doughnuts door to door on Saturdays with my brother, did other jobs as well as took on a full time job in a restaurant when I was 14 as a dishwasher—to make money for "luxuries" like my camera, film for my camera (I took all the family photos),

fabric with which to design and make clothes (when we couldn't wear pants/jeans because it was against the rules in junior high, I tailored my own clothes), etc.

As a young adult Joy knew poverty of her own; more recently she enjoys comfort and even luxury. But all these realities harbor the uncertainty that alternating between having and fearing not to have can create. She concludes that

> certainly not having money and having it have both marked my life. I remember nearly starving in Oklahoma as a young mother, as well as my mother's own struggle to make money. I panic when I'm short, and it starts affecting my self-image. I feel "worth-less." When I have a fat bank account, all my bills paid, I feel more powerful and vow never to get in a position [like the one] I am in now: with checks due me and no money in the bank. I "have money" though, now . . . as well as the ability and opportunity to make more. When I didn't have it I couldn't eat out, had less mobility. When I was a student with two children I rode the bus, walked everywhere (including to the laundry with the clothes on my back), and when I went to [a] restaurant, which was rare, I often had to choose between the jukebox and a coke. The jukebox often won out!

Gwendolyn, an African American assistant professor of literature in her early thirties, doesn't want her daughter to have to suffer the pressures that shaped her childhood. These had their origin in her own parents' determination that their daughter have access to opportunities a racist society had denied them. Her father came from first-generation northerners; he studied medicine and became a prominent surgeon by always being the best: "Second best wasn't enough. It had to be best." Gwendolyn's mother was the youngest in a family of entrepreneurs. She used every bit of her wisdom, initiative, talent, and willingness to sacrifice in support of her husband's and daughter's well-being. The degree to which each succeeded became the relevant mark of what her family, and she herself, might become.

This dictum that nothing less than the best is enough stressed Gwendolyn's early life and continues to influence her relationships, including her relationship to money. As a child, she was taught that everything had a price: "You had to be prepared to pay that price . . . which often meant planning way ahead, in ways no young person should have to anticipate." She married an historian, quite a bit older than she, more established, and white. He was supportive of her finishing her Ph.D. after they got together and has helped her financially as well as encouraging her intellectually and emotionally. She believes her upbringing made it more difficult than it might have been for her to accept his help without discomfort or guilt. But Gwendolyn's greatest concern is for their little girl, now four:

> I probably don't need to be thinking this far ahead, but I want her to feel freer than I felt as a child, less constrained. I mean, she's going to have a bundle of problems as is, being a child of an interracial marriage. . . . But I'd like her to grow up with a more realistic approach to money: where it comes from, what it is for. If it's scarce, she can worry. But if it's there, let her enjoy its possibilities. I was always so uneasy as a child, really afraid. It's not always clear where race ends and economics begins, or vice-versa.

In response to my questionnaire, I was fortunate to receive answers from several generations of women in a single family. These gave me an explicit look at generational trends. The following are from a grandmother, mother, and daughter who is herself a young adult. Mary was born in 1919. Her daughter Glenna is now in her late forties. Glenna's daughter, Jean, is in her mid-twenties. These women are from a long line of Catholics, people who earn their way working for others, with fewer offspring as the generations unfold. A sense of community and mutual aid remain important.

Mary writes of coming into young adulthood during the Great Depression. Money issues were approached obliquely. Her father was the sole earner, and her mother "worked hard to get money from him . . . by any means she could. She asked directly ('Glenna needs new shoes') or by getting us to ask ('Ask your father') or by going thorough his pants pockets while he was sleeping." During that difficult time her father kept his job, but the family also took in boarders. She remembers that she

> never had objective data on [the] family's financial situation. . . . I
> knew money was scarce and was warned not to talk about [it]

outside the house. The three oldest—one girl, two boys—did seem to be part of the family counsel, but 'us [younger] girls' were not included for a long time. When siblings got jobs, they were taken over by Dad with advice on how to behave in business situations and money matters. But he himself wasn't good at saving.

Mary's daughter Glenna says money was handled carefully in her childhood. It was discussed in terms of practicalities and being frugal was a value. "I think there was a subtle message from my dad that girls were more expensive than boys," she remembers: "I felt pressure to buy inexpensive clothes and he griped about the cost of makeup." The messages Glenna received clearly influenced her later sense of self:

> Because I was taught you had to work for what you got, I thought nothing of having to work when I left home. [But then] at 18 I married a working-class kid who didn't manage money at all. It was my first encounter with a "spend it while you have it" mentality. I opposed it the whole time, *but adopted a feeling of lack of control around money that I didn't shake for a long time.* (my emphasis)

Glenna is now in a lesbian relationship in which her partner and she have separate accounts, "which is a mutual agreement that works for us." She makes more, so their arrangement is a 60%/40% sharing of expenses. (This is common today among women who make homes together. Usually a household fund will receive from each a monthly deposit commensurate with her earnings. Beyond the prorated sharing of basic expenses, each woman may also maintain a personal account.)

Glenna's daughter Jean is conscious of the ways in which she has internalized the money messages handed down from her grandmother's and mother's families:

> I feel that the class in which you were raised is more often an indicator of the ideas you have, the people you feel comfortable with, [and] where you "hang out." I think money is a bigger barrier than race or culture or anything else.

She says she is "sometimes uncomfortable in nice restaurants or rich homes," that she's "never gotten past a first date with someone with money." And she remembers: "I once went [with a guy] to a restaurant in a rich neighborhood. I asked if my date was okay with the prices and he became insulted."

Jean also talks about her struggles with her boyfriend. She says they have been together for four years and keep their money separate in terms of checking accounts and rent and bills, but that when they need something they don't keep track of who pays for what; when one of them is broke the other helps out. However, she admits they have one issue with money that arises from time to time:

> I work full time plus many hours of overtime. He works 30 hours as a T.A. and goes to school. There are gaps in his employment, and I make up the difference. During these times I feel he should do more around the house. It is always tilted in his favor when it comes to housework. He tends to clean more than me, but when he's unemployed it bothers him and he feels taken for granted. I work my ass off and feel that *this* is taken for granted. We have yet to find a true solution, but we're trying. We usually talk it out, then he begins work again and we're both busy and life goes on.

Life goes on. The average man's involvement with the unpaid labor of the home is still nowhere near as generalized as women's entrance into the paid labor force, albeit at the lower end and with fewer opportunities for moving up. The above response, from a very young woman, reveals that in the mid-1990s and among fairly conscious heterosexual couples, a real shared responsibility for the home is far from easy.

Patriarchy and capitalism combine in our society so that most women, irrespective of class, race, or other determining factors, grow up with a lack of knowledge about where money comes from, how to manage it, and in fact *what it really means*. This makes the myth-making easier and the generational damage more difficult to define. In the making of this book I've been privy to stories which seem to illustrate a broader than usual spectrum of the fear, misuse, and resultant attitudes which in one way or another affect us all. Breaking generational strictures then becomes harder, sometimes quite traumatic. Such is true in the following story, and I will quote from it at greater length.

Ellen is a professional woman, a writer and motivational speaker, who confesses to having spent a great deal of her life "learning to have, spend, talk about, enjoy, and not feel confused about money issues." She is from a middle-class Jewish background, 43, and married. Like so many others, she begins by saying she felt

> "average" as a young child, assuming that everyone lived pretty much like we did. I don't know that I would have become quite as conscious of differences in the size or quality of people's homes, cars, furnishings, etc., except that my father was constantly comparing himself against other people . . . [and] my mother had an overwhelming sense of superiority toward just about everyone unless they exhibited a significant amount of wealth. . . . She is still quite impressed by money.

A single story, one of many, sums up the attitudes that helped shape Ellen's childhood: "I remember one time," she says

> when I was about seven or eight, maybe younger. My father was bringing us home to New Jersey from a visit with relatives in Philadelphia. Before driving up to the toll booth, he pulled the car over and stopped. "Do either of you have a nickel?" he asked. Now why in hell would my younger sister or I have thought to have brought money along. . . . Both she and I panicked, thinking we'd have to spend the rest of our lives on the shores of the Delaware unless someone forked over the bridge toll. No doubt my father was trying to "teach us the value of a dollar," but this experience did little more than scramble both my sister and me for quite a long time.

Contrary to other respondents, Ellen believed she understood her family's financial situation; her parents fought about the subject constantly. The secrets and lies mostly followed shopping trips with her mother: "She'd take us shopping [and then] often come home and hide what she'd bought." Whether the purchase was for herself or the girls, it was important that Ellen's father not be told:

> Here is the way it was supposed to work. My father was supposed to earn all this money and my mother was supposed to do all the house stuff and be free to spend as she wished. . . . [She probably] handled the money, [but] there was this "rule" where the wife had

to ask the husband's permission. One of the big conflicts was that my father never gave permission gracefully, but always made my mother wrong for wanting to spend, even [on] groceries [or] shoes for the kids.

Anxiety was fueled by talk of never having enough, or verbalized worry about where the needed money would come from. "I was so paranoid," Ellen remembers,

> that whatever I got, with very few exceptions, I banked. No shit! I had gotten the message very early that spending let alone enjoying money was really evil. Although [I never spent] more than tiny bits here and there (even in high school). I rarely bought more than school lunches. I had little freedom to do anything.
>
> I do remember starting a secret savings account when I was about 13 or 14, to save up for my parents' 20th wedding anniversary, which would have occurred when I was 17 had they not gotten divorced a year earlier. My sister and I put $2 of our $3 weekly allowances into [that] account for a couple of years. After the divorce, we spent the money on a life membership to Hadassah for my mother, which meant a lot to her. It never would have occurred to me to use that money for myself.

The message, for Ellen, was that money meant survival and security; although she knew that neither of her parents really felt secure, regardless of what they had. They attempted to teach their daughters the value of money by lecturing them about how poor they had been when they were younger, how lucky their children were by comparison, or simply by arguing. Ellen doesn't remember ever being held financially accountable for anything: "The time I broke a neighbor's window playing softball, either the neighbor's insurance covered it, or my parents paid."

> This was all kind of paradoxical. We had money, but there was always this sense that we didn't, probably because of my father's chronic state of panic and the constant arguments. Since, according to my father (and to this day, his family), my mother was this out-of-control spending machine—which I sincerely doubt she was— and my sister enjoyed shopping and spending like my mother, I took on the role of family savior, thinking that if I went without, maybe some of the conflict would ease up.

Of course that never happened. The roles we are forced to assume as children, in response to problematic family dynamics, rarely fix anything. What this particular situation did to Ellen was cause her to adopt a "not wanting" mode that has followed her throughout her life. "As an adult," she says,

> I remember going shopping and often coming home with something a little less attractive or less expensive, something a little below what I really wanted. I've worked through a lot of my deservingness issues and have no problem buying for myself today. In fact I've recently had to start looking at setting up a little more rigorous savings and investing program as I've sort of blown that off for a number of years. Feels like the pendulum is swinging back to center now, but god it's taken a whole lot of work to get here.

Ellen and her husband have been together for 21 years. At first they kept their money separate. She has most often been the primary wage-earner, which she sees as backlash against her mother's dependence. "I never wanted that kind of a relationship with anyone," she says. Gradually, they merged their finances, and now share bank accounts as well as decisions regarding larger purchases.

> We do not fight about money. I had enough of that in my childhood to last me into my next 80 lifetimes. However, about 12 or so years ago, my husband called me on a tendency I had, to go out and buy something and then bitch about spending, or come home and panic. He couldn't handle that, and asked me to either spend money and enjoy it, or not spend it. A reasonable request. Realizing I was indeed channeling my father, I copped to that habit and swear I've never done it since.

As is true of most professional women, Ellen has suffered the attitudes of colleagues and others who believe our gender justifies their trivializing or taking advantage of us in business. When she was negotiating her second book contract, a male editor tried to talk her into a flat-fee contract without royalties. Patting her on the hand, he urged "But dear, you'll be a published author!" She says men have often told her that women don't know how to sell, can't close a deal, don't know how to negotiate. "I'm constantly walking this fine line between holding onto some level of integrity," she sighs, "and going after what I want without resorting to the worst, most bullying kind of male energy. Some days I do better than others."

Ellen has worked hard to change the attitudes she inherited. The panic with which she grew up is never far from the surface, but she's been able to rise above it. One last story speaks of this struggle, and how it can change the person imposing the distorted values as well as the one making the break.

> One of the most liberating moments in my life was when I was in college. My father, who decided I wasn't paying enough attention to him, threatened to cut me out of his will. He also said something about never sending me money again. But by this time I was working and on scholarship; I really did have a big thing about not being financially dependent on anyone, and was willing to do anything, live any way necessary, to maintain my independence.
>
> I don't remember him sending me money [after that], the entire time I was in college, except for one check for $75 and a graduation gift a few years later of $1,000. [The changed relationship] blew his mind. And talk about panic! He figured he'd had a lot of leverage . . . and then there was none. It was a wonderful moment for me, and ultimately taught him that there were a lot of other ways to connect with his daughter.

Generational patterns of behavior build upon themselves until why we feel what we feel and act as we do may be lost in a thick haze of coverup and shame. A language of justification is invented and the myths take over. Changing our attitudes and the way we act upon them can clear the way for healthier responses, healthier living. In this struggle for change, though, we must remember that the lies, secrets, and silences are embedded in our histories. In the next chapter we will see just how deeply and how intricately embedded.

From Shame to Resistance

4

The Money Lies

> I strained my ears. . . . Daddy was telling . . . how he had always been the one who provided the money in our family. . . . I stood there in the dark and listened to Daddy tell lie after lie after lie. It wasn't true, none of it, and even . . . the youngest had eyes and ears and a brain enough to know what Momma did and how she worked day after day.
>
> —Nina Simone

> What are the tyrannies you swallow day by day and attempt to make your own, until you will sicken and die of them, still in silence?
>
> —Audre Lorde

What about the feelings money or the lack of it promotes? It's not only the broad generalities—that having money can make us feel secure, while not having it may produce endless anxiety, fear, even illness. Or that growing up with an overabundance can make us feel we cannot be loved except for our money. Or that hardship engenders thrift and frugality, while opulence may produce generosity—or, more often and interestingly, a wary avarice.

We learn our own particular set of attitudes about earning, having, saving, spending, and pass these on to our children and others over whom we exert some influence in ways that may feel confusing to others, invasive, or even threatening. Money lies of different types become routine.

Strange behaviors can become the norm. Gretta is a widow with substantial economic assets who sends birthday checks to her children but not to their spouses—because she doesn't like them all and "wouldn't feel right giving to some and not to others."

This woman's practice would seem to be about meeting familial obligation while avoiding giving to those she dislikes. But in the process those she does like lose out as well. Her "solution" is an expression of Gretta's inability to act upon genuine feelings of love or appreciation. Her parents taught her well that appearances were what mattered, everything had to seem equal or fair, and unruly feelings best be silenced. Now an arbitrary fairness standard forces her to decide at the lowest common denominator, denying those she really does love and limiting her ability to make a spontaneous gift.

And this is only one of the many games this family plays. "Don't tell so-and-so I gave you this" may accompany an otherwise routine gift. This is the lie by omission. From one generation to another, acts of great generosity have been tainted with requests for secrecy which, far from making the recipients feel special, burden them with a sense of guilt or shame. Family members are conditioned to perpetuate this behavior until they cannot be sure of what may be said to whom. In time the imposed distortions become their own.

Pam is 30, Yonsei or fourth generation Japanese American, and married. She describes her class as middle-middle, then laughs and adds: "Is there such a thing?" The following story is one I have heard frequently, even experiencing one of its variations myself. When money is allowed to stand in for love, certain lies are cultivated. Complicity is offered, or demanded, as a requisite to belonging. Pam says,

> In my family, money meant affection. My relatives all sent Hallmark cards for every occasion with some cash. I had to write thank you cards for each and every one, but without being so crude as to say how much I had received. In college, my father showed me that he was thinking of me and cared . . . by sending envelopes with money (no letter) and I knew he had won the football pool, couldn't tell Mom that he had gambled, [or] was thinking about me and was giving me some illicit free cash to spend without accounting for it to the family.

Here we have gifting that is not to be spoken of directly; it being crude to mention the amount received on cards of acknowledgement which are nonetheless expected from childhood on. Money is an expression of love, and bonding involves a secret "pact"—in this case with father against mother, but even more often with mother against father, or in any other configuration that tends to enable and protect behaviors that do no one any good. As Pam continues to reminisce, she produces another story that includes its own faked responses and is still more telling in the way it measures caring. It is also culturally interesting in that it contains a particular ritual of ethnic tradition.

> When I was young and went to visit older relatives, they always gave me money. Whether it was a quarter or $20 (it depended on the relative and what tie we had), we had to act like it was totally unexpected and unwanted. [Only] after careful protestations was it accepted with both sides not losing face.
>
> The twist on this scene is that I was very close to my grandparents compared to the other grandchildren. There was a little piggy bank in their room [and] at the end of the visit they always prolonged the goodbyes by saying, as if they had just remembered, "Oh, go get the bank and bring it here. I don't know if there is anything inside since the last time you came, but we'll see." I would always be wondering if it was heavy with pennies or quarters and at the same time hate myself for being so greedy to even think such not-so-nice thoughts. By the time I returned with the bank, which was very heavy, my grandparents would have a sack (literally a cloth sack sewn with double seams) and we would open the bank and start counting it all out.
>
> Now that I am older, I wonder why the whole ritual of counting. Was it for me (to measure my worth) or for them (to measure the extent of their affections for me)? My other cousins received pennies, nickels, etc. I never mentioned what booty I scored to anyone but my mother, so I don't think my cousins or aunts and uncles are the wiser, but I do know that I somehow had warranted some unspecified amount guaranteed.

An elaborately contrived performance, in which lies, secrets, and silences all played a part.

Some of my narrators' stories thinly veil dramatic dis-ease, revealing the rarely explored connections between the power wielded by money and that which is perpetrated by sexual or other forms of abusive control. Myra is a dancer and community activist in her early forties. She is from a working-class family of eastern European origin, all women. Her father disappeared early on, leaving a grandmother, mother, one sister, and herself. Myra was married, had a son, divorced, and now lives with her son and long-time male partner. She remembers:

> Money was rarely given to me. I earned it as soon as I could think of things to do in the neighborhood and then of course through massive babysitting. . . . I remember feeling from an early age that I never had enough money for treats. [And so] I began a process of regularly taking change from my grandmother's cigar box where she kept her tips (she was a waitress until she retired at 72). I realized that I was doing something wrong but was able to rationalize my actions by the fact that I was spending lots of this change on others in the neighborhood and on some candy for my schoolmates. The loss of her tips became visible as I increased my handfuls and I was eventually discovered. My mother was horrified, my grandmother was deeply sad and angry, and I was scared. I don't remember either of them talking to me about how I felt. They did ask me why I did it and then they brought the church minister into it and I became mortified, fearing that everyone at school would know. *I remember this as a particularly dark time and parallel some of these actions with the incest I was experiencing then.* (my emphasis)

Indeed, I have found that the secrets kept and the lies told about money invariably touch upon other areas where women are forced into guilt and shame becomes a necessary refuge. Feelings nudge and piggyback upon one another. The lines between them blur. Where one area of vulnerability ends and another begins is probably less important than how unhealthy attitudes about the various issues can rob us of self-esteem and prevent that independence which can lift relationships from a plague of repeated imbalance.

As discussed in Chapter 1, we don't talk easily about money—especially within a family or with close friends. And so the excuses and cover-ups develop, as well as the silences, secrets, or outright fabrications. Almost everyone who responded to my questionnaire listed a few financial lies—committed, or by omission. The following is a representative selection:

"I only talk about [money] in a depersonalized way and to *some* people.... I tend to underplay what I have as I tend to identify with women [who are] 'have-nots.' I've been trying to analyze why I do this and I think it's a form of camaraderie or way of bonding with my sex. There is also some shame in having something if I feel others don't."

"My mother has a small account ... and my brother does not know about it. It makes me feel very uncomfortable, since both his family and mine pay for her apartment. Her relationship with my sister-in-law is not good, and I think my mother is afraid that [she] is going to take [her] money away from her."

"I sometimes say things cost more or less than they actually did, depending on who I am talking to. I am silent about how much I owe on my credit card, which I keep using despite resolving not to. I pretend I have more money than I do, and thus spend too much."

"My exact money situation, I think, is my business, but I'm not aware of telling lies about it. I don't pretend that I'm suffering from lack of money, but ah ha!—perhaps I let people *think* I have less than I have because: 1) I don't want them to be jealous or resent me, 2) I don't want them to feel they can take advantage of me, 3) I'm afraid I may be embarrassed by having more than many of my friends, [and] 4) I don't want there to be any temptation for someone to like me *because* of my money."

"I don't like to admit to how much we have, how much [my husband] makes. I downplay how much we pay for things. I ... have a superstition (which I hadn't really articulated in a long time, until this question) that the money I have will roughly equal the money I need. This used to seem to hold true in a very literal sense. If I got a gift of $100, it was almost for sure that one of the kids would need a doctor visit, or the car would need tires. It worked the other way too. If I had to buy [my son] a new soccer uniform, I'd almost magically get an extra on-the-side typing job offered to me. This superstition causes me some trouble now that we are beginning to have more money than we spend every month—it feels like it invites disaster. Surely one of us will have an accident, or the house will burn down. Something."

"I have most recently experienced the death of my partner's stepfather as an issue of serious secrets. In fact, I received this questionnaire on the day I returned from a week with his mother, helping her put [her dead husband's] clothes in order. There is a great deal of money in this family. While I was there I saw some figures that were staggering. The amount was not the issue for me, but the degree to which it has been kept silent blew me away. When I shared this story with my partner, we both decided to also keep it quiet and I don't even know why!"

"My best friends and I share emotional and sexual secrets and our most intimate thoughts. But we have never told each other what we earn. We never ask. I fear to ask my friends who work in the same institution with me, because of the possibility that jealousy will come between us, and resentment."

"If my husband asks how much we have in our checking account, I always tell him at least $100 less."

Joyce, a white woman of working-class origin who administers a not-for-profit political organization, writes:

> Secrets? We have $1,000 in savings and tell everyone we don't have savings. This is our "real crisis" money, and we hope never to have to spend it. I don't know why it's hard for us to admit we have a savings account when it is . . . so small. I guess because in the process of deciding about sending our daughter to college, finances were a major part of the decision, and in talking with people we told them how hard it was going to be and didn't want them to think we weren't telling the whole truth. In general I'm very open and honest. So it feels strange to me to have this secret.

These habits of concealment and these fears of vulnerability are easily traced to the ways our parents dealt with money issues: what they told us and how, whether they used or abused us in the process, and particularly the ways we were made to *feel* when victimized by practices leading to fulfillment or denial.

Sometimes the tension between a father's need for control and a mother's desire to soften the contours of family life and make things okay for her children produces amazing contortions in the woman: secrets and silences that become an integral part of family life. Grace is a TV producer in her late thirties. Her family was upper middle class, belonged to southern white society, and had a history that must have seemed much more unusual to her than it was:

Money in my father's house was completely controlled by him. I remember my mother telling me that my father's father married my grandmother, who was 16 years his senior, "because she was a good investment." She was comparatively wealthy, and my grandfather took her money and made his fortune with it. I grew up in a comfortable style; I was educated in private schools, my parents had a summer home. But my father was a contractor, and if the housing industry was good we lived well. As that industry began to wane, our lifestyle was modified. Nevertheless, he controlled the purse strings, and meted out the pennies to my mother as if he were her employer. He was also somewhat abusive if we spent money that did not concern him. Steaks for dinner were fine, but spend the steak money on a new dress for me or my mother [and that was] cause for a huge row. Clothes that weren't hand-me-downs were always removed from the bag, tags clipped, and smuggled into the house. We bought most of those sorts of things when my father was away and incorporated them into our lives as if they'd been there forever. [Because of all this] I never felt comfortable with money. I grew up seeing it as a means of patriarchal control.

Rebecca, a professor with Jewish working-class roots who remembers class as the unspoken theme of her childhood, ponders on some of the money secrets she finds herself keeping even now. In the process, she makes some interesting connections between class and race—and shame:

[With] friends who are working class with few chances for upward mobility, I'm shyer about discussing my privilege. [For example] I have a white gay man cleaning my house every other week. I don't tell that to everybody, especially friends of mine who clean houses because they are illegal or unemployable. I do feel embarrassed. Is it easier for me to hire a white gay man than a person of color to clean? Absolutely yes. Less racist stereotypes for me to face as a white person with middle-class privilege. Do I tell everyone I had a black cleaning lady? Not everyone. Yet I do tell people that my working-class elderly parents have two third-world women as their health care workers, and that they get meals on wheels and are applying for Medicaid.

I don't have shame about my parents now. I almost feel proud of their survival and mine. But I do have shame about them exploiting poor black women as cleaning ladies. Mary cleaned for them for 20 years. They knew very little about her. She stopped coming one day; I'm sure she died. They never knew what happened to her. They had a number to call and never got through. My mother is mad at Mary and has no consciousness of how separate their lives were.

Jane, the artist and graphics designer in her mid-forties, remembers the money secrets of her suburban, middle-class childhood:

Finances were banned from polite discussion . . . other people were not supposed to know our financial status. I was reprimanded by my mother once for telling a phone caller that my dad was out of town, because "people might think he's looking for a job." In fact, it was his job that took him out of town periodically.

Speaking about her life today, Jane says that

the greatest secret I have about money is that I lie to myself about it. I don't look at the facts. Like time, I figure there's probably enough of it. There often is, there frequently hasn't been. I don't review my books, or make a financial plan, going month to month. If I'm nice enough and do good work, the clients will come.

Jane's attitude mirrors that held by many women, who have been conditioned to believe that ignoring a possible trouble spot will keep it from erupting. Denial may produce the illusion that a problem will go away until an accumulation of denial explodes in our faces and we are left wondering if there might not have been a better way to address the problem.

Battling the fallout from a complex web of family secrets and lies—about money and much else—has kept Jane from being able to make healthy decisions about business, art, and family or allowing these different areas of her life to support one another as they otherwise might. Perhaps ironically, surviving cancer in her early forties forced her to rethink the causes and effects. This is proving to be the experience of a growing number of women who, when faced with their own mortality, find it possible to cut more quickly through disabling conditioning. And, like many, for Jane it's been a long and sometimes contradictory process.

Cherise is a young black woman, a recent college graduate who is taking a year off before going on to a Ph.D. and what she hopes will be a teaching career. Of Jamaican origin, she was born and spent her early years in Pasadena, California, where her parents owned and managed properties. In this family the lies and secrets were less the product of parental withholding than those that come with the territory when there are unexplored issues of race and class. Racism and the differences between those who own property and those whose lives they control remained unexplained and therefore mysterious to Cherise:

> My mother was the housewife who handled the accounting end, lawyers, the banks, and investments. My father left every morning to go to the properties which they managed ... truthfully I do not think I seriously connected the properties, which were such a part of our daily lives, with a paycheck. I was comfortable. We were comfortable. We lived in a nice house, had two cars and a dog. I knew that our tenants were generally poorer than us, but that was not significant.

Cherise's large extended family of aunts, uncles, and cousins were also poorer than they. Her parents helped buy clothes, pay medical bills, even provide piano or swimming lessons for those less fortunate family members. But her mother became ill and died when Cherise was seven, and several of these same aunts and uncles managed to get their hands on the family money then, almost sending her father into bankruptcy. He was able to continue to raise his children with privilege, but was profoundly affected by this disloyalty on the part of his wife's siblings. And he explained it in detail to his daughter, who says she therefore suddenly "knew from the age of seven my family's financial situation."

In Cherise's youth, what she remembers as being most confusing was that "no one seemed to work." She found it difficult to explain to her playmates what her father did or "why my parents own 'your' house ... suddenly 'Mr. Boll's child' had a nasty ring to it." At a certain point, Cherise was sent to a rich, predominantly white, private school. Suddenly comfortable became ordinary. And when she visited the palatial homes of her friends, what had been an overabundance became poverty. I became very ashamed of my house and more embarrassed of my father who constantly wore blue overalls, the same overalls that I fought and cried to get not even eight months before, until my mother made my brother and me a pair. It was a schizoid existence until we moved home to Jamaica.

On the island where Cherise's parents were born, race faded, color gained in importance, class leveled out, domestic abuse entered the picture, and a hard work ethic became the primary marker:

> Though we were upper middle class, we were raised as if we were poor. My father's decree [was] 'I will not do my children the disservice of spoiling them.' This meant that I learned how to work, clean, wash, build wood and coal fires, work outside, care for the cows and dogs. All of these jobs were ordinarily performed by the scores of workers attached to the homes of the middle and upper-middle classes. My [new] reality combined with my skin color and abuse, [and so I] shared these issues with darker-skinned people, the majority of whom were/are poor. [This] made me feel very uncomfortable.

As with so many others, in Cherise's story the lies, secrets, and silences could be felt in the disparity between appearance and reality. Rich was suddenly poor, ordinary became rich without warning, racial considerations influenced perception, and abuse rearranged it all. She naturally gravitated towards other girls who, for different reasons, also found themselves straddling lines of class and color. They talked about their lives, calling themselves the "middlers." And they consciously opted to "move independently of the class-color stuff, but if made to choose, chose the lower or darker side." Today Cherise says,

> to a far extent this helped me reconcile many of my issues. I was an outsider and I understood why. College was a whole new chapter. But essentially my feelings about money were set [back] then. I understood money as a tool. You are supposed to save and work hard. Money was a shared affair. You should be your own boss. Never follow the Joneses. Spend on the important things. Frivolous things will pass away and leave you poorer. Watch the cents and the dollars will take care of themselves. A curious mixture of privilege and insecurity.

In Angela's childhood the lies and silences were also traceable to issues of race and class, but they were further complicated by the fact that she was adopted. Angela is in her late thirties, American Indian, an enrolled member of the Seneca Nation at Cattaraugus, New York. Born to a mother living in reservation poverty and with other children to support, she was put into foster care at the age of three. She spent the next 15 years with this family: white working- and middle-class people of Irish, German, and Scotch descent. For Angela, money secrets were intimately linked to her condition as an outsider:

> I did not understand my family's financial situation. Money was not discussed freely. I had no idea what the foster care payments amounted to, what my father's salary was, or what my mother earned on her part-time jobs. I had no idea how much our monthly budget was for household expenses. I kept secrets about my father's gambling and my mother's part-time jobs because the family thought that [the truth] would jeopardize the foster care license.

Unjust systems often demand that we lie in order to survive. It is not only the unhealthy attitudes inflicted upon us as children that prod us to measure our responses; we may also lie or remain silent because telling the truth would be to our obvious disadvantage in terms of eligibility, support, security. Women, oppressed under patriarchy and capitalism, learn early on that a lie is sometimes the most expedient, or only, course of action.

Angela grew up with a strong work ethic; "Money seemed to be something that people had to work very hard for," she says. It also stood in for love, and giving it seemed to be the only way her foster father was able to express his affection. She inherited this work ethic, to the degree that she has felt "supremely alienated from my peers. . . . I have often been criticized and even ostracized for making those who work less hard 'look bad,'" she admits. But the mixed messages of her childhood also nurtured another sort of imbalance. She explains:

> I have recently overcome a huge debt created in the early eighties. I used a credit card to the limit and then found for nearly ten years that I could barely make payments to cover the phenomenally high interest. I learned many things about myself, others, and the

predator credit card companies in the process. I am very proud that I did not succumb to the easy way out of declaring bankruptcy. However, I do wish that there were some way to punish the credit card industry other than to never use them again which I can only do on an individual level.

Issues of race or class denial do not have to cloud a child's perception of where she comes from and who she is. And money handling doesn't have to be a battlefield. It depends on how forthright parents are able to be, whether easy logic or a web of lies is the backdrop to family interaction. Usually it unfolds somewhere between the two extremes. Clemencia, a Mexican American writer, teacher, and political activist now in her mid sixties, insists that "one cannot speak about issues of women and money without speaking about class and labor issues. These inter-relate with gender mightily." She draws lessons from her parents' lives, from how theirs have impacted hers, and how her life has affected her daughter's.

Both Clemencia's parents were of lower-middle-class Mexican origin who in time moved into the North American middle class. Because they were teachers of Spanish—her father in the university, her mother in a high school—they survived the depression and were able to save enough to build their own home. She remembers them both speaking often about that house as something they would leave to her so she wouldn't have to worry about her own security later in life. Their attitudes towards money were careful, precise, and open:

> [They] saved, and only later in life could travel considerably, worry less. My father did very detailed recording of expenses in ledgers. They both gave a lot of thought to planning ahead. For example, my mother did extra studies so that she could qualify for the highest possible pension when she retired.

Race was nonetheless an issue. Clemencia speaks about the ways in which it played out in her family:

> What I don't remember is how moving to an all-white neighborhood was possible when my father was a dark-skinned Mexican. Probably because he was, at the time, working at the Mexican Embassy, and therefore had status as a diplomat. . . . I don't

remember being taught that poor was "lazy." With a Mexican father we had enough of that stereotype around. My mother did maintain "charity" practices, at Christmas and on other special occasions. She made small donations from the 1960s onward, to the United Farmworkers, Native American causes, etc. My father sometimes showed an attitude toward workers who came to the house that I didn't like; he would be polite and friendly but do small things that told me he saw them as inferior, especially if they were black. This surely had something to do with being very dark himself, and considered black at times, e.g., by a busdriver.

Clemencia's main financial memory is that her parents didn't have enough money for her to have her teeth straightened, the one thing she remembers really wanting as a child. Yet she had dancing and piano lessons and other middle-class advantages. She was expected to get a higher education. And her parents have been generous in providing financial security not only to her but to her daughter as well. At times in her life when she chose political activism over a secure job, her parents gave her

> two credit cards . . . and I could be sure they would pay the bills when I couldn't. . . . These were for necessities, no big flings or trips. But still this kind of security had an influence on me and my [being able to choose] political work for very little pay. From 1964 to the present I have never had a "straight" job, except for about nine months. My parents [also] provided a sense of security for my daughter. . . . They paid for her education or clothes at different points when I couldn't.

And she adds: "Probably for this reason there have been problems I can remember between my daughter and me over money."

Problems arise, even in a family where the tradition of money handling has been so straightforward and generosity from generation to generation apparently easy. Secrets replicate themselves in every conceivable scenario. Fiona is an elderly woman, still working, who describes herself as a successful, practicing school teacher and administrator. Years ago she also worked as a bookkeeper and office manager for a real estate company. She admits that this means she has been able to manage financial affairs for others, but says "I am secretly terrified of managing my own finances. My strategy as the head of household and provider for family, and a single woman, is to work hard for a regular income and to receive and spend it with as little attention as possible . . . writing checks until the money is gone." She says she never admits to any of this and only her closest friends suspect it.

A few years ago the Internal Revenue Service where Fiona lives offered to prepare simple income tax returns. She jumped at the offer, but it turned out to be an experience that deeply marked her. The IRS made a mistake, showing a much larger salary for that year than what she actually earned, and therefore inadequate withholding. Even after hiring a tax expert, Fiona could not obtain a copy of the return they filed on her behalf. She went through such agony during that period that she has been unable to prepare her own tax returns since. She says she has protected her misadventure with IRS "in much the way I keep any health problems secret."

Marjorie is in her late forties. She is white. Her family of origin started out working-class and ascended; she describes them as "climbers. We always had the least of anyone who lived where we lived. . . . I never felt I understood the family financial situation. Money was a 'secret topic'; it was impolite to ask about specifics." Examining her own money secrets, Marjorie says:

> [They] have to do primarily with my beliefs, I guess. I usually lie by omission about how much I (don't) earn. I have learned that respect comes from a title, but can be demolished by a salary. . . . If I am with people from whom I feel I need to gain respect, I hide my slum address. I don't do these things with my friends, with the people I trust—but I tend to bristle and evade when they ask me things like "How much is your rent?" or "How much did you pay for that blouse?"

The lies women are forced to tell, even to their husbands, often have a poignant side. Rachel, a musician and the faculty grants officer at a private liberal arts college, is a middle-class Jewish woman in her early fifties whose mother and father, like so many others of their generation, never managed a completely communicative relationship. She tells the following story:

> When my father was months away from death, he received a notice from the engineering firm for which he worked, saying that he

would no longer receive a salary but that the company would continue to pay for his medical expenses. My mother intercepted the letter and decided to confront the company officials, citing his more than twenty years of service. She was aware that if the salary were cut, my father would feel useless and give up hope. She must have been very forceful. The company carried my father until his death. Of course Dad never knew of her mission.

Lily, a white woman in her late forties, married and with two college-age children, has recently gone back to school. In another year she will be a lawyer. Her origins are a fundamentalist Christian family in which, she says, "money always seemed very tight. There were five children and my father was a public school teacher. My mother was a great sale shopper with both food and clothing. To this day her name is Bargain Bessy (also Bible Bessy, depending on the context)." Money secrets are a part of Lily's early memory. "I don't remember my parents arguing about money," she says, "but they did argue about income taxes. My mother would refuse to sign the form because she felt my father was doing [something] illegal. . . . He would agonize alone over bills and taxes."

Later, in speaking about how she and her husband have dealt with money, with their children, and with one another, Lily explores her own secrets and lies. She handles family finances, pays the bills, does their taxes, and generally makes the decisions about what to spend and when. Her husband prefers not to be involved. Lily describes him as "a very hard worker [with] expensive tastes in food, clothes, and entertainment." She tends to be "more conservative and plan long term. The main lie," she says,

> is that we're broke all the time. I am a student but my husband earns a good income. It doesn't provide enough for us to move out of the ghetto and own a home, but that is more because of the way we choose to live than because we are shut out. If we lived on a tight budget and scrimped for a down payment and then a monthly mortgage, we could buy a home. But we know from the past that a tight financial situation puts more pressure than we want on our relationship, and have chosen not to live that way. We pretend we cannot change our living situation, but the truth is we are afraid of that commitment and pressure so we stay where we can be more comfortable.

Lily also notes:

> I think that I play the poor role with my children to avoid saying I
> don't want to spend for [something]. Instead I say we can't afford
> that. It's easier but not honest.

"I can't afford that." How many times do we say this, when what we
really mean is "I have the money but prefer to use it for something else."
Or "I'm afraid my choice may seem selfish to you, and I depend for my
self-esteem on what you think." Or "I have not learned to defend my
own decisions, so I'm telling you I just don't have it."

Clemencia explains this further. She is the Mexican American woman
quoted before, whose parents were so careful of money management as
their daughter grew but were enormously supportive of her choices as an
adult, even to underwriting her political activism. She is not entirely frank
about money but, in contrast to those who are all but unconscious about
the lies they tell, is very clear about what she chooses to say to whom, and
why she will not share certain aspects of her financial situation:

> I don't tell actual lies but I perpetuate vagueness if not silences.
> This concerns some modest financial resources I have from my
> mother. I may mention those resources in general terms, but not
> the precise amount, which might sound like a lot to someone
> younger who has no idea of what it would be like to actually live
> on my $400 Social Security check in San Francisco—where my rent
> alone is almost $700; or how they tend to treat a person if she is in
> a nursing home on Medicaid; or how quickly you can go through
> thousands of dollars if you are old and sick; or other chilling aspects
> of growing older with limited resources. So if I say "I can't afford to
> go to that play for $50 a ticket" it is vague, since I have, for exam-
> ple a $25,000 CD. Obviously I could cash it in and have that $50,
> but such an expenditure just doesn't fit into my overall attempts at
> basic financial security as a single woman living alone with no one
> who could afford to help me in case of problems. I'm reluctant to
> call that a lie. Or is it?

It may be a lie. But not the kind that results from manipulative conditioning, or from Clemencia's need to control those dependent upon her
honesty. Rather, this is an example of how the larger web of social

distortion does not encourage real honesty. We are made to feel it is easier to lie than to explain ourselves.

How important do most of us believe it is that our language accurately reflect the truth of our experience? Certainly it may be argued that small lies spoken to save someone's feelings or to achieve a "greater good" are justifiable. Still, they so easily become part of the fabric of a greater social lie.

What does it say about our culture that in order to feel comfortable with one another we lie as a matter of course? What does it say about our ability to know ourselves and others that so much of our communication and interaction depend upon a series of fabrications? Our entire human exchange is kept off balance, making it easier to accept and believe the skewed discourse that bombards us on TV. Or is it the other way around, our inability to discern reality spawning the TV patter? Certainly this weave of personal and public semi-truth produces a complex discomfort, which may easily result in a situation like the following.

Verna is a white woman in her early forties, the assistant manager of one of the outlets in a nationwide sporting goods chain. She and her husband, a writer, have moved several times in as many years, always pursuing better job opportunities for Verna. She has only recently begun to speak about deeply rooted money issues which have clearly plagued her for years. Now they surface in troubling ways:

> I have quite an emotional barrier about money. A resentment that I don't have more, guilt that I "want," and a hard time feeling close to people who, very obviously, have more of it than I do. It's just been in the last three years that I've started to make a salary that I could actually support myself on. John's and my joint financial situation has improved somewhat, but not as much as you'd expect because my career advances have been at the expense of his. And of course he makes some of our income wherever we are.
>
> As we've gotten older we're both aware of letting our lack of a nice home and "things" interfere with potential friendships. I feel embarrassed over our inability to accumulate "stuff" as if it's a very visible symbol of failure. The janitorial firm that cleans the store [where I work] is owned by a couple that I was becoming friendly with . . . [and] I invited them to come visit.
>
> We had fun and enjoyed them. Then they invited us over. And they had this beautiful house with a landscaped backyard with a

little pond and more outdoor furniture than I have inside my house and this incredible set of copper pots and pans that they cooked us dinner in. Sally, who started her [own] company and works incredibly hard, was very poor growing up. George, her partner, is used to having plenty of money and things. I enjoyed them both, but I was slightly uncomfortable all night. And I have not been able to invite them back to our house.

Verna finds it difficult, even painful, to socialize with people whose economic status is higher than hers, or whose ease with what they have contrasts sharply with her own uneasiness. Here another silence is born. Until she is able to deal with what is unresolved in her own experience, she will probably avoid this couple who could have been friends. And they will never know why.

Some of my narrators went more deeply than others into the forces that shaped their families of origin, allowing us to see how behaviors were constructed, truths were bent or lost entirely, lies were born, and conditioned responses became the norm. New York poet and philosopher Susan reiterates that we "can't separate the issue of money from how we feel about the first people we saw involved with it and how it affected them." She emphasizes that our memory is always shaped by the fact that children don't see things in a context. When we're small we don't know the categories we later learn to put things in. And she adds:

At the same time, particularly for those of us over forty or fifty, childhood may not be the main causal factor—what my parents did, who they were, may not be as important as who I am, what I have done in my thirty-odd years of adult life. In my own case, living as a lesbian since the age of 21, for much of the time alone, supporting myself since the age of 20, along with more than a decade of difficulty finding work because of my leftist politics, certainly has had as much or more to do with my relationship to money than my primary relationship with my parents.

Like so many, Susan's class and cultural background is complicated. The secrets, the lies, would become clearer to her only as she grew into her own sense of the world. Her parents came from immigrant families— Russian and East European Jews—for whom survival often depended upon silence. They both wanted and feared assimilation. Notions of escape and the eternal search for security—pogroms, the Holocaust—were indelible markers:

> Both my biological mother and father were children of immigrant parents who spoke little or no English. . . . Neither of them ever spoke of their backgrounds. I believe my mother's parents were from around Kiev in the Russian Ukraine, and I had always thought my biological father's were from Poland until he claimed that they were from Lithuania—that's where he thought the more "sophisticated Jews" were from. Neither one of them really seemed to know for sure, which is one of the main reasons an exploration like this is so difficult and complex. My grandparents didn't talk to their children, and their children, my parents, never communicated to me that simple but important information about their own lives that most people take for granted. I don't even know my grandparents' names.
>
> It is next to impossible to categorize these people according to traditional notions of class. My grandfather, on my mother's side, was a teacher. My grandmother, a seamstress. When they came to America, he couldn't find work teaching, so she taught him her trade and he became first a tailor and then a clerk in a drugstore. My biological father was an auctioneer. None of them lived in or brought their children up in traditionally American middle-class or working-class homes. They were displaced culturally, educationally, and economically. When my mother and father married, he was a salesman in a department store. They were divorced when I was four.
>
> My stepfather was an immigrant who came to this country from Russia when he was five, left home at the age of 15, went to Atlantic City, worked as an actor, a script boy, and then began to manage vaudeville acts. The theater was one place open to Jews. He had a third grade education. None of my family ever went past high school. My stepfather eventually went to Hollywood in the late thirties, where he became a very successful actor's agent.
>
> And my mother married him. For money? For glamour? For attention?
>
> [Someone once] characterized me as coming from a family of assimilated Jews. In fact, they never assimilated. I thought at one point they wanted to fit into "American society" but now I think I was wrong. They were transplanted Jews. All their friends were Jewish. The neighborhoods we lived in were almost all Jewish. The

high school I went to was overwhelmingly Jewish. [My parents] both spoke Yiddish fluently and didn't trust anyone who wasn't Jewish.

Money, for them, meant security. For the Jews in Russia and Eastern Europe at the beginning of the century, or in Europe in the thirties or forties, if you were perceptive or lucky enough, it provided a way out. If you got caught, money made little difference. For my mother, it meant a new kind of escape—escape from the grinding poverty she grew up with as a child of immigrant Jewish parents who didn't speak the language and worked in menial positions. An escape from the grayness and brutality of her childhood. Money colored the surface of her life, making it bright and glamorous. She and my stepfather were, after all, the looked-down-upon "nouveau riche." They spent their money. They lived it. They didn't save it. They wore it.

And what did they teach their children? They could spend a thousand dollars on a sofa and complain about giving out a quarter to us, for fear we would get "spoiled." In hindsight, I believe the way they were treated as children, even though their economic circumstances became vastly different, was the way they treated their own children. I was pampered at five, but by seven was wearing hand-me-down clothes.

When I was a child, I see now that my parents used money as control. A child lives, for the most part, in a world without alternatives. And money is dealt with within that context of which we are unconscious and of which we can only make sense after the fact.

Although I wasn't aware of it then, I must have connected money with my parents and their lifestyle. And rejecting their lifestyle and them, I . . . rejected the pursuit of money—perhaps to an extreme. However, I like to think of what I have done in my life more as being pulled toward the things I respect and admire than as rejecting what I disliked.

I was and continue to be ashamed of my background. Even now I am reluctant to talk about where I came from. It is really rather ironic. My parents were ashamed because they were poor and never spoke of their background. I am ashamed because they had money and hardly ever speak of mine.

The only reason I talk about it now is because I feel it is important to strip away the manipulative illusions of Hollywood which are being used to veil the reality of the world we live in. Hollywood is a world I know well. I grew up knowing the truth of it. My stepfather had to be in touch with reality to succeed—unlike the actors he represented who all too often began to live their parts.

I have never been interested in "making money" or in having the kinds of jobs you needed to have to make a lot of money. Which might not have anything to do with my childhood, but rather with what I chose to do with my life: become political, be a poet.

I believe now it is a mistake to try to fit things into cubby holes. With the issue of money, class comes up. But, as I learned in Spain, class is not really a question of money, it is a question of education, cultural background, expectation.

My parents were not looked up to because of their money. They were respected within their own circle because of the quality of my stepfather's work. He was intelligent, relentless, and ruthless, and he was the best at what he did. But show business is hardly a respected occupation among the elite and to the average middle-class and upper-middle-class American of his generation, he was, when all was said and done, just another flashy Jew.

Like the one above, some of the stories confided to me possess such a broad array of gendered and other cultural money codes that I've wanted to offer them more fully, exploring their complexity as their narrators have. This is especially true when poverty, alcoholism, and abuse conspire to shape a woman's secrets and silences, her attitudes about having, keeping, using, and spending money. Here is another, very different, story—one that is riddled with silences and contains terrible secrets.

Sue worked for the Milwaukee Railroad for many years, making locomotive wheels, rare for a woman. She comes from poverty and has known it to varying degrees for most of her life: in two marriages and through the rearing of five children. Nearing midlife she began to come out of the suffocating cocoon into which oppression so often thrusts women. She lost her job with the railroad and fought a successful battle for severance benefits. She writes and publishes powerful poems about her working-class origin and woman's experience.

Sue suffered the death of one of her sons. She had endured her father's murder of her mother long before. She and her second husband eventually moved West, and she started working as an advocate for other blue-collar women. She has sought therapy in order to deal with the terror of her childhood, and continues to write and publish.

Sue's response to my questionnaire was stark, vivid. Reading it, I knew that hers was a personal essay waiting to be written.[1] She describes her first memory of money as

> nickels, pennies, dimes, and dollar bills, cash and coins flying through the air and crashing to the kitchen floor all around my mother. And me? I was unimportant to my father, and to my mother apparently. Neither said "hold on, Suzanne is here. Let's handle this later." That would have been the rational, nonalcoholic approach. I hid beside the doorway with a five-year-old's eye view. Somewhere in my mind I remember thinking I was being on my mother's "side" by staying there instead of running away. . . . I was "used" to the fighting and my father being drunk.
>
> My father had come home drunk, (again) late and had cashed his welder's paycheck as usual in the tavern on the corner. [My mother] asked for some cash for groceries. He said she was nagging him again. He swore at her. He lunged at her. She backed away. He proceeded to throw the money *at* her, not to her. She picked it up, put it in her apron pocket and went to the store. My father went to bed. I don't remember what we had for supper that night, but I know I ate it.

Sue extrapolates from this story to the atmosphere of her entire childhood:

> Sometimes, when I was really hungry and supper wasn't happening, I'd take bites of a raw potato from the cupboard shelf. I also ate radish sandwiches, bacon grease spread on bread, and a lot of jelly sandwiches. We didn't have milk or cheese on a regular basis. We had chicken soup on Sundays when my mother was able to get part of my father's paycheck.
>
> I was trained to know the difference in the meat market between soup chickens and other chickens. Soup chickens were old and tough and fat and had to be boiled a long time. You couldn't bake or fry them. Baked chickens were special. Not Thanksgiving. We didn't have it. Not Christmas dinner. We didn't have it. My mother made flour and egg noodles and put potatoes in the chicken soup. I loved it.

Sue elaborates on the desperate ruses her mother was forced to devise in order to secure the money to care for her family. "My mother would try to hide money from my father," she explains, she would take it out of his pants like a thief or a whore while he slept. I would see her. She would put her finger to her mouth and shush me so as not to wake him up from his drugged sleep. Unfortunately, she would hide it so good she couldn't find it herself. She would cry and beg me to help her. . . . I remember hunting, with her sobbing quietly, digging through couch cushions looking for her little change purse.

In Sue's early life, money was power. She saw how it was rarely shared with women, but sometimes with other males. Although her father frustrated her own early attempts to get part-time jobs and help out, he did allow her brother to work and there was some sibling solidarity. She remembers that her father didn't know it, but her brother would let her come with him on his paper carrier route and when he collected trash:

He needed someone to help hold the load from tipping over. I helped dig the scrap metal and newspapers out of the alley bins, and I'd walk/run alongside the coaster wagon holding my hand on the top of most pieces. Sometimes they'd shift suddenly, and I had a hell of a time keeping it balanced. My brother would give me some of the money that the scrap man gave him. It was our secret. So I discovered that some men gave you money if you did something for them, but it must be confidential.

Sue's pain was determined by poverty and by who held the power. "Because my father abused me mentally and physically," she says, "lack of money was only a tiny part of the pain and lack of power." What she has managed to change in her life is the role money plays and how it is handled in her primary relationship. Her description of the process is, again, compelling:

I now have a decent job with good pay. The kids are grown and on their own. The man who shares my life also shares the power of money in our family of two. Even so, in the beginning I needed to have my own bank account. We pooled all his paycheck and 99% of mine and lived off of that. But for at least 15 years I had a small account that grew slowly to $432.00. Finally, I decided that I could trust him. It didn't seem to matter any more. I bought what "our" money would allow. We made decisions about big purchases: a new car, etc. He doesn't "tell" me I can't buy this or that. I don't tell him either. We don't have money secrets. We don't tell lies about what we spend money on, although I must be honest: once in a while if I buy some piece of clothing I don't really "need" I don't tell Larry right away. He doesn't spend money on clothes. He doesn't care about fashion. Why do I not tell him? Old habits die hard I guess.

For women, secrecy and silence can mean many things. Sometimes they constitute a conscious strategy in a world where we live in such disadvantage with regard to male privilege. At other times they may be almost automatic. They may have been our only possible resistance in early situations of abuse, nurtured in times of great vulnerability and maintained as habits that are difficult to break.

Lies inevitably result from intense feelings of shame. Whatever the reasons for our secrecy, silence, even lies, there comes a time when we learn that continuing to perpetuate them begins to do us more harm than good. To avoid educating ourselves about money, to shy away from its management or gratuitously hand it over to others, to continue to let shame and ignorance stand in for openness and honesty, can only keep us down—and damage our relationships with those we love.

In the next chapter I will look at wealthy women, those whose abundance, not poverty, has forced them to juggle with different—but nonetheless overwhelming—equations of shame, guilt, dis-ease, and responsibility.

The Wealthy Woman 5
Money versus Power

> Americans need to transform rich women into witches,
> evil stepmothers, criminals convicted of no crime except
> that of using their money (or what they thought was
> their money before some man claimed it) in a public
> way.
>
> —Sallie Bingham

> Women with wealth and women without wealth share a
> sense of isolation, alienation, powerlessness. We feel this
> way no matter where we are . . . people like me need
> people like you, and people like you need people like me.
> Together we make a wonderful whole.
>
> —Byllye Avery, Founder
> National Black Women's Health Project

Most of us at one time or another have sighed, "If only I were rich!" Our conditioning encourages us to believe that the single lucky hit will bring it all: happiness, self-esteem, the ability to feel at ease in our bodies, even the perfect relationship. If we are poor- to lower-middle-class women in this society, we may have been raised to think we could acquire the necessary wealth by marrying a man with money or by striking it big at some sort of gamble: the lottery, bingo, a Publisher's Clearinghouse prize. Pitifully few of us were educated to expect financial success from our own creativity, personal business acumen, or skill. Many more were socialized to believe that our economic salvation lay in marrying a rich man.

Then there are those women born into money. They have never known anything but its privilege—and its problems.

In twentieth-century North America, women are the recipients of a fairly complicated set of messages about our relationship to money. We are taught that we shouldn't really put it first. After all, isn't love more important? And health? And loyalty? Certainly we shouldn't learn how to manage it and "don't have the head for it" in any case. There is something inherently dirty and shameful about too much money, particularly about flaunting it. Yet there seems to be a price tag on everything we need or want.

If we do not have money, we must seek it quietly. If we have it, we must hide the fact.

In "The Masculinization of Wealth,"[1] Gloria Steinem draws upon her memories of "them and us." Them, in this case, being the rich girls in the midwestern town where she grew up. "It was," she says,

> a world of difference marked by possessions. Between Saturday night movies and winter vacations; weekly pay envelopes and checking accounts; Easter outfits bought on the layaway plan and designer clothes ordered a season ahead; social security checks and stock dividends; kids who slept on sofa beds and children with nannies; in short, between an envious life and an enviable one.

In the forties and fifties these rich young girls were unquestionably white, a fact that did not need to be stated. Today most but not all of them still are. In her essay, Steinem explores the ways in which having money or not having it affected the young women and men of her childhood. The wealthy young women were being groomed for wifedom, of course; to oversee the homes, produce suitable heirs, and entertain for the wealthy men they were expected to marry. If physical appearance was on their side, and they managed to master an appropriate demeanor, even young women without money might aspire to "marry up"—the female version of the American Dream. As Steinem puts it, all these less wealthy young women needed was "the magic moment of being chosen."

Poor or middle-class girls also aspire to marry money. Several industries have been built on nurturing such dreams—from the adult romance comic to the TV drama, popular film, the so-called women's magazines, and many other purveyors of the myth. Boys, on the other hand—even most of those from the wealthy families—didn't generally worry if they "married down." Steinem describes this as "a power difference that only enhance[s] their male role."

Girls from monied families, of course, are expected to marry men of similar or greater wealth. If their fathers own businesses and there is no male heir, a son-in-law may be groomed to take over before a daughter is considered, quite apart from the skills of either. Gender speaks louder than intelligence, experience, even interest in or aptitude for the work involved.

Traditionally, favoring men over women in matters of money continues throughout life. In the wealthier families, the trusts set up for daughters are quite different from those established for sons. Even in such cases where the actual amounts might be the same, availability and access are usually not. It is assumed that women will marry men who will care for them; men will have to care for themselves and, at least on the paper surface of "the American way," their wives and children as well.

The daughter of a well-known film star responded to my questionnaire with a painful and perceptive life story. This excerpt is typical of how even one relatively sophisticated father differentiated between his daughter and his son:

> Every time my brother and I go to the estate lawyer on business, the man only speaks to my brother. He believes me to be incompetent and when he is forced to speak to me he condescends. This despite the fact that it has been me and not my brother who handled the entire dismantling of the estate and that I am the only person who has any idea what is going on with it. My father [also] conveyed his lack of confidence in my financial abilities to the lawyer in the form of the trust documents which are far more restrictive of me than of my brother. The lawyer has incorporated my father's attitude into his own limited ideas of the competency of women. (I have known the man for four years and he still hasn't bothered to learn my correct name.) I am constantly struck by his blatant sexism, and yet it is far from blatant. To him, it is the most natural thing in the world.

This gender differentiation creates interesting patterns, largely invisible to other people and even to some of the women affected. What is socially accepted is not seen as problematic, and traditional practice generates its own distortions. Men who are heirs to their own family wealth tend to trade first wives in for women who are younger and prettier and thus better able to adorn their hearths and client dinners. Midlife crisis is the term that has been coined to describe men across class lines who, when they reach their late forties or fifties, replace first wives with younger women. Corporate CEOs and other business tycoons, however, may feel they need the younger and more glamorous women to fill a very specific social role.

If the business has descended through the wife's family and a man begins to think of divorce, he will often wait until his father-in-law dies before discarding the woman who so amply endowed him. Popular discourse has women sleeping their way to power, while a look beneath the surface of the myth tells us it is much more often the sons-in-law who do so. Ex-wives, in such divorce settlements, are more likely to receive monthly payments which are far more limiting and controlling. These often stop if the women remarry and do not readily facilitate starting over.

The women are being punished for reneging on a contract which clearly stipulated loyalty, service, and a lifetime guarantee. Steinem quotes one such divorced wife, also a student of economics, who claims that "the national total of [the] large settlements given to sons-in-law [is] greater in any given year than the total amount paid to women in the much-resented and publicized form of alimony."[2]

One of the central conclusions of Steinem's essay is that "The closer women are to power, the weaker those women have to be kept."[3] We are familiar with the techniques used to keep women weak: one in four of us (by many accounts, a conservative estimate) is sexually abused, frequently by a family member and at an age that ensures lifelong vulnerability. In recent decades the numbers of women who literally starve themselves into taking up less room has also risen dramatically. The incidence of anorexia, bulimia, and other eating disorders seems to increase among women of greater financial means; these are eminently white and middle- to upper-middle-class plagues.

And then there is our rigorous programming for service. This built-in mechanism of control crosses class lines. It is common to all women in our society, from the poor to the very rich. But for the rich the programming is not about making a pot of chicken soup or coming home from an exhausting job to an exhausting basket of shirts to be ironed. "We are supposed to take care of people, especially men" says Sallie Bingham, whose own life has been a map of what happens when a very wealthy woman rebels against that mandate. "Women do not challenge corporations. Women do not cause discomfort to millionaires," she writes.[4]

Passion and Prejudice is Bingham's memoir of her early years and of the events that would so dramatically change her life. Daughter of the family that owned much of the state of Kentucky and molded the opinions of the inhabitants of that state through its influential web of media properties, Bingham's life unfolded in all the luxury and promise typical of her class and gender. In other words, she was entitled to the comfort without the control, the opulence without the decision-making, in short: the money without the power.

Perhaps because she lived at a time when numbers of women were beginning to make the connections that open doors to change, and certainly because she possesses an unusual store of perception, wisdom, and courage, Bingham challenged that most sacred of all American cows, the family. Hardly an ordinary family, hers was an extraordinarily rich one, where patriarchy and capitalism are linked at their most manipulative. She saw racism, sexism, and mismanagement in the family businesses. She sat on the boards of those businesses; why not speak out? Why not, indeed. The Bingham women were expected to sit on the boards precisely so they would *not* speak out. Their task: to protect the male interests as if they were their own.

Bingham became a feminist. And an excellent writer. Her struggle was a long one, involving much personal pain. Her punishment for not only attacking her family's power but also telling its most closely guarded secrets was swift and thorough; she was banished and disinherited. Still, she was able to force the sale of the empire and to use what she could of the $62 million she eventually received as her share to establish a foundation for women artists. Some of the rest went to lawyers, some to taxes, and half remains tied up in trusts drawn up by her father and grandfather!

Bingham's story is unique in a number of ways, but it is also part of a trend among conscious and courageous women of wealth who are putting their money to work to challenge patriarchy where the stakes are highest. This is not an entirely new phenomenon. What's new is the trend—incipient organization, national meetings, a network—and the fact that women are beginning to talk and write openly about their money, even when they have a great deal.

A few wealthy women of vision and courage have historically been able to use their fortunes to further causes in which they believed. Mary Ellen Pleasant, unnamed in conventional history, helped fund the abolitionist struggle.[5] Alva Belmont, a southern heiress, supported the National American Woman Suffrage Association. Mrs. Frank Leslie left $2 million to Carrie Chapman Catt, one of the leaders of women's suffrage, although half was eventually siphoned off by over-ambitious lawyers. These women, like Ann Hess and Jenny Warbug almost a century later, were exceptions. Today there are organizations such as Resourceful Women, that offer support and encouragement to women managing wealth.[6]

Genevieve Vaughan is one of this growing number of wealthy women who have fought their way out of the position into which women with money have traditionally been kept. She established the Foundation for a Compassionate Society, "promot[ing] and validat[ing] women's values at a level from which they have often been excluded ... long term change as well as ... intense immediate needs such as ending nuclear testing, power, and pollution, protesting wars and arms production, and providing some relief and solidarity to victims of war, especially those resulting from [our country's] masculinist interventionist policies."[7]

Vaughan has written an interesting position paper explaining her foundation's philosophy. Parts of "Women's Giftgiving" are worth quoting as an example of one woman's thought processes as she moved from dutiful (wealthy) wife to someone in conscious control of her own resources. Vaughan's paper begins with a couple of lines from Mao Tse-Tung: "The revolution is not a tea party / The revolution is not old ladies making lace."

"Fortunately," she responds to that male bastion of Left political doctrine, "feminism has now validated our telling our own stories, thinking our own thoughts." And she proceeds to tell hers, interwoven with the questions, and eventual answers, which she, as a very wealthy woman, began to ponder about male and female attitudes towards patrimony, whether in the form of possessions or ideas:

I had read Malinowsky in college, on giftgiving among the Trobriand Islanders, and Marcel Mauss's work on gift "exchange." These anthropologists talked a lot about reciprocity. But couldn't the bonds be created without reciprocity, simply by knowing someone else had satisfied your need, or by becoming aware of someone else's need and satisfying it?

Simple enough questions, and reflective of the best—the healthiest—aspects of the female care ethic. Vaughan draws on her experience with her three daughters, noting that as a mother she fed their needs, not the other way around, and that mother and daughters had bonded with one another through this process of need satisfaction. She also understands how men traditionally have gotten women to do the caretaking. "When I read about Levi-Strauss's ideas on the exogamic exchange of women between groups of men," she says, "it occurred to me that what these men were exchanging were free givers, gift-sources."

Vaughan sees money as standing in a one–many relation to a group of things, products. And she notes there is

such a proliferation of one–many structures it [is] easy to think of them as "natural": . . . the king to his people, the patriarchal father to his family, hierarchical military, religious and business structures, money to commodities, even the city to the country, the owner to his/her properties. . . . Each . . . set[ting] up a rivalry.

In contrast to this she envisions an entirely different system, one based upon satisfying need rather than establishing control:

It began to seem to me that there were two logical movements which were co-existing though conflicting with each other. It stood to reason that those who followed logic of ego orientation would not easily recognize the gifts of those who were other-oriented. Seeing themselves as the source of their own well-being would reinforce their position of power, and seeing others as that source would diminish it. . . . I was curious about how and why this happened and for many years tried to understand what the connections were between exchange and the formation of the dominant ego. (Another way of asking this might be "What is greed?")

In offering her ideas on what many have called a care ethic, Vaughan goes on to explore male and female language, how our socialized positions affect the ways in which we speak and how the ways we speak define who we are:

> by feeding back the form of the definition into the definition of gender, thousands and millions of times, we have created the many self similar images which riddle our society, and which feminists have learned to identify as "patriarchy."

Genevieve Vaughan assesses her position as a wealthy white woman in the United States, privileged because she is "more comfortable and [has] more access to education, travel and possessions than most of the people on earth." But she is also clear that she is

> not in the one–many position in the same way wealthy white men are. It is not part of my role to take the place of others, dominating them in order to be in the one position. Instead, I am myself part of the many when relating myself to men, and my marriage was traditional enough to make it normal for me to be almost one of the children.

Vaughan founded an organization which she directs "by right of being the one who is the funder," although she insists that she tries to let other women lead as well, while communicating "the vision and the practice of the gift economy." And she closes by affirming that

> this is my answer to the quote from Mao—though the ladies who are doing [the gifting] are not old. Yes, the revolution is women breaking the barriers, having tea and talking with each other. Yes, Mao, the revolution is all women making lace.

Women who inherit money are not expected to use it in ways that challenge the patriarchal structure. They also must not reveal what they may learn about the ways men buy and sell other human beings, wage wars of greed, murder when necessary, destroy reputations, or prevent advancement in order to maintain the status quo. The secrets are sacred. In "What Came After," a 1991 addition to her memoir, Sallie Bingham speaks of her family's panic at her revelations, and how she was able to make peace with what might otherwise have remained a painful isolation.

We are formed by our families, and only by breaking away at an early age (preferably before eighteen), taking drastic action to learn a skill, and engaging in years of therapy of the most eclectic kind do we ever become whole and sane enough to seek those people, surely not blood relatives, who can be our friends.[8]

Steinem quotes Bingham talking about her use of a fortune she all but lost: "I give out of rage, rage that there is never an end to giving . . . [and] rage that I didn't use to believe what I gave was mine."[9] She describes some of the difficulties inherent in stepping away from inherited wealth and all the confines that wealth sets in place. "Apparently, we need our rich," she writes, "certainly we are willing to make sacrifices to support them, as our tax system shows."

Bingham knows better than most that "power is the core of the dispute." She also knows about the role creativity can play, and how art can generate power of another, more enduring, kind: "To write is to have the impudence to claim that I have something worth saying. To write is to lay hands on the tools of patriarchy, not the pretty plumed pens but the missiles—the adjectives and verbs and nouns that change minds and sometimes even change people."[10]

Taking back the power has many faces. Writing is certainly one, claiming or reclaiming the voice. Others may require the proverbial room of one's own. A woman may have to decide to eat enough to stay alive, learn to feel comfortable with the space her body occupies. Or leave a relationship that doesn't work, not stay in such a relationship to avoid social disapproval or "for the sake of the children." Perhaps she will go back to school many years after she's "finished." She may change careers. Or remember and deal with abuse. For a woman with inherited wealth, taking back the power undoubtedly means gaining real control over that money which was supposed to be hers and then using it to challenge the system that keeps all women down. Affecting change in one's own life always means remembering and reclaiming the stories, then learning to inhabit and pass them on.

Interestingly, recent studies indicate that the *perception* of male ownership of this country's wealth is not supported by actual figures. Sixty percent of the wealth in the United States is actually owned by women.[11] Advertisers certainly know this; witness the proliferation and variety of ads aimed at female buyers. The number of women-owned businesses grew by 20% in 1992, to a total of 6.5 million. In the same year more than $79 million was raised for women political candidates running for House and Senate seats, only $10 million less than their male opponents received.

Of the 3.3 million Americans classified as the richest by the IRS in 1986, more than 40% were women. On average, the women in this group were 6% wealthier than the men, held slightly more corporate stock, and were considerably less in debt. This last comparison is particularly noteworthy, for it tells us that, contrary to popular misconception, women are good at managing money.

It also seems clear that women's care ethic crosses class lines. We already know that poor or middle-class women, whose collective memory of poverty always remains vivid, are more likely to look ahead, spend only what they have, and avoid overabundance or waste. In spite of the fact that they are stereotyped as frivolous and compulsive shoppers, they may shop compulsively for the little things, but men make the big expenditures. When women do take charge of their finances the more positive aspects of the care ethic often surface. While men will go into debt to acquire the toys that proclaim status, women tend to think of those less fortunate or design programs aimed at changing the power dynamics rather than simply dispensing charity.

Patriarchy has had centuries to become entrenched and refined, and it requires courage and creativity to challenge what has become an obstacle course of dangers. Women have been well trained to defer to male views, not to make waves, in fact to consider themselves fortunate in those tradeoffs in which they are cared for in return for service and subservience. But a quarter century of new feminist agency has made complex inroads into this destructive culture. It has challenged women to ask questions. And there are palpable signs that among wealthy women the balance is beginning to shift.

One example: in estates worth $5 million or more, 48% of female decedents, versus 35% of male decedents, made a charitable bequest in 1986. Men who inherit wealth are more likely to invest it in business endeavors. Women often have a different vision. Another example: although women's colleges make up only 2% of all colleges and universities in the United States, they account for five of the eleven institutions that raised the most money from their alumni per student enrolled in the academic year ending in June 1990.

Women are not generally seen as sources of great wealth, so even if they do have access, its gendered management often prevents them from understanding they may be capable of administering it in ways that benefit themselves—and other women. But the same studies cited above tell us younger women will form the financial core of social-action advocacy movements in the next decade and that these movements are already heavily female—three out of every five members are women. Almost half earn more than $50,000 annually and 60% are professionals and executives. Considering the impact of feminist thought on younger women particularly, change seems likely.

As we come to understand the *potential* economic power women hold, it's important not to lose sight of the fact that this country's poor are *overwhelmingly* women and the children they support without help from men. There is a relationship between the very real feminization of poverty on the one hand and the masculinization of wealth on the other; the former is a direct result of the latter. Changing family patterns may also affect our earning power and the way we spend.

More and more lesbian couples are deciding to have children. Unmarried heterosexual women consider motherhood as well, something almost unheard of several decades ago. Single motherhood, as a category, no longer only denotes a divorced, abandoned, or victimized woman. Choice has entered the picture. We may well be talking about a mature lesbian couple consisting of two professionals who have consciously decided to raise a family, not a single teenage girl who became pregnant because the conditions of her life offered no alternatives.

Whatever the family model, Steinem and others remind us that women and their dependent children make up 92% of those on welfare, and that female-headed families account for most of the working poor "while the gender of those who control this country's great concentrations of wealth is even more uniformly male. It's simply not possible to attack one ghetto without also attacking the other."[12]

We need to look beneath the surface of this apparent contradiction. More than half our country's wealth is owned (if in name only) by women. Almost half of our wealthiest citizens, according to IRS statistics, are women. Yet our poor are in the vast majority women and their dependents. The feminization of poverty is real and growing, while at the same time women who are wealthy or even comfortable are moving to greater ownership of businesses, endowment of social programs, and the realization that they can learn to control more of what they have and to use it more creatively. Nothing explains this contradiction but the lingering power of patriarchal control, if not always exercised through actual financial ownership, then generated and reproduced in the attitudes that continue to matter.

Women born into wealth must confront a particular set of obstacles in learning how to manage their money without arrogance or shame. They occupy positions of such obvious material comfort and fulfillment, it is often difficult to begin to question the paradigm. Kit Tremaine is one of the new group of female philanthropists. Louisiana lumber heiress, poet, race horse breeder, once Queen of the Mardi Gras, and tireless homeless advocate (as well as contributor to many other causes), she writes: "[I had to] struggle to be an adult after coping with being born into a wealthy family and then enduring childhood. It's hard to grow up."[13]

Hard to grow up. Much harder to throw off the blanket of justification that makes living at the expense of others acceptable. And if one does manage to break through the curtain of lies and semi-truths, and if—more dangerous yet—one decides to do something about it, to make a meaningful change, punishment is immediate. Sallie Bingham describes this well when she speaks of her family's response to *Passion and Prejudice*.

The Bingham family spent an estimated half million dollars to commission and nationally distribute a book of its own, an eleven-pound refutation of the story Sallie told. She says that "at first, being publicly attacked brought on numbness—the shield of the survivor . . . and then laughter."[14] But powerful men know that our most vulnerable identity is our voice, which we have quite literally created from under the weight of millennial silencing. Bingham admits it was

> different when they attacked [my book]. . . . To attack my integrity as
> a writer endangers my survival. . . . It was about guarding secrets,
> keeping lies intact, protecting the reputations of some pretty dubious
> men. . . . The attack was against the truth: against naming names,
> telling stories, and putting women back into the spotlight—dragging

them back, if necessary, from early graves. . . . It was an attack on the right of a woman—any woman—to tell the story of her life.[15]

Again, the importance of the stories. And these are no longer simply about what happened to passive recipients. Increasingly they are also about women as active protagonists—how they use and give back what they have been given, how they take what they need, and change the options available to those who come after. With a conscious sense of self comes agency, replacing dependency and submission.

Among the responses to my questionnaire on women and money there were several from women with inherited wealth. Jana, a fine photographer in her early fifties, was born in Texas into a wealthy Jewish family. Her story reveals the contradictions as well as the satisfactions:

> I always knew there was enough money for anything I wanted. We lived in a small, three bedroom house until I was seven . . . but then, in 1949, my parents built a huge English Tudor style two-story house. . . . I knew we were different.
>
> I didn't always like being known as the richest. I knew that my mother didn't give me what I needed from her, and [I] didn't like being driven to and from school by the chauffeur, whom I made drop me off and pick me up a block away.
>
> My mother was tight with silly things like postage stamps. She was the frugal one in the family, though she spent whatever she wanted. Daddy was the spender/showman. . . . I wasn't kept out of discussions about money, but I knew that I would never be expected to earn [it] and my brother would, even though our trust funds would have the same amount in them.

Jana is absolutely clear that she is "who I am because I have always had money. It is no more separable from my identity than if you asked 'has being female marked your life in some fundamental way?' I am also other things, but fundamentally I am a monied Jewish woman artist!" At the same time, her relationship to her wealth has undergone changes as she matured and felt the necessity of matching attitude to ideals. She remembers:

> When I was married, [my husband] was a lawyer and made a good salary. He handled all my investments and kept my property sepa-

rate because my father turned over all my assets to him when we married. I was 19, the trust matured two years later, and [my husband] handled it all. He even paid all the household bills except for the maid. We spent only what he earned, rarely invading my income. My parents had given us our first house so we had no house note to pay. We paid cash for cars and everything else.

When I began working I paid the bills which involved my photo expenses, but still he took care of everything [else]. As my independence grew I wanted to begin paying all household bills but he would see them stack up (I paid them bi-weekly) and it drove him nuts. He liked paying a bill the next day, so he took [the job] back. When we divorced I realized right away that I would never feel as secure again, even though I had plenty of money, I would never again be taken care of that way. Sometimes I long for those times, but only in this context.

Although Jana's son and daughter also inherited wealth, expectations and tasks underwent generational differences. On the subject of helping around the house, and being paid or not for such participation, Jana remembers:

I was never paid for any household tasks, and did none. When I took off my clothes, I dropped them where I was, and the maid picked them up the next day. I never made my bed or did anything at home. I never worked, never had a paying job, even for summers or Christmas vacations as did my friends. [However] I did not do this with my children. They had chores, [the] responsibility to keep their room clean, but they did not have to make their beds or do their laundry. They did things like feed the dogs, help clean up dinner dishes.

Jana's son is a rabbi, her daughter in retailing:

[Their] careers . . . are important to them, they like being paid for their work, and they supplement their earnings with their own [inherited] money which allows them to do pretty much whatever they want. But they do not live lavishly at all. My parents set up trust funds for them at birth as had my grandparents, so my children have been independently wealthy for years now. I continue to give them yearly gifts as the tax laws allow, and they will inherit my money. They already inherited from my mother because I encouraged her to skip a generation on my side, which my brother did not, of course.

Jana's life partner is now a woman. Esther has always been comfortably off, but her assets are nowhere near Jana's. They live according to Jana's holdings, and this has not always been as easy as Jana's money relationship with her children, who have always known wealth. About money in her primary relationship, she writes:

> It hasn't been easy, but we deal with money well now, after some amount of work on it. I could never try to be in a relationship with someone who has a like amount of money because that narrows the field too much, at least with women, and since I am a lesbian. I have my separate property, Esther has hers. The agreement we have reached is that she contributes all her income to our joint checking account, and I contribute the rest in order to pay the bills. Sometimes the expenditure of money gets sticky when Esther wants something I don't want. Sometimes I act with her like a person who has had money all her life. It's okay for me to decide to spend money on the things I think are important like taking the Concorde to Europe or buying some art or piece of furniture, but landscaping??? But she was right, as usual!

Jana speaks most poignantly to the way having money has impacted her life when she admits:

> Money and love are synonymous to me in this way—I used to think I could be loved for my money. That is, I thought I didn't have other lovable qualities but surely I was nice enough and someone could see how much better/easier their life would be with me. I am the great fix-it woman, and money is a big part of that. But now I see that I can be loved for who I am, and that sometimes money gets in the way of living to a great extent.

Victoria is younger than Jana, and her family wealth was accompanied by Hollywood contradictions rather than those embedded in a wealthy Jewish community in Texas. Victoria, too, has an older brother, though, and some of the same gendered differentiations and expectations applied.

She remembers her earliest sense of the role money played in her life:

> As a young child, prior to my parents' divorce when I was eleven, I
> have no conscious memories about the way in which money was
> handled. We lived in a mansion in a very wealthy area of Los
> Angeles and I went to a private school where many of the other
> students were "celebrity kids" as well. I was aware that those of us
> who were children of famous people were regarded as somehow
> different, possibly even "better" . . . although not necessarily more
> popular. But that had less to do with money than with status. For
> example, Clark Gable's son was in my class and he was regarded
> with some awe, although he was a bit of a troublemaker and not
> particularly bright.

The desire to downplay wealth seems to have been there even in this
film family, in a community where ostentation and glitter are an integral part of life. Even as a young girl, Victoria experienced the contradictions:

> My family was less ostentatious than many of the other families, it
> seemed to me. There was a great deal of conspicuous consumption
> at my school, and although we had a huge house and a Rolls Royce,
> my mother was always quick to point out that she had done every-
> thing in the house herself and that my father had been given the
> Rolls instead of being paid for a job he had done. Nonetheless, we
> only traveled first class and stayed in good hotels. As a child I
> remember being very blasé about money. The woman who did our
> laundry used to try to get me to respect it a bit more by threatening
> to keep any cash she found in my pockets.

Then, as happens also in families of much lesser means, divorce
changed things. The confusion continued, made more complicated by
the fact that two homes were now involved:

> When my parents divorced, everything changed. My mother had a
> very difficult time getting credit cards and although the divorce
> settlement was sizable, she became very cautious about money in
> her daily life. Simultaneously, however, she was beginning to
> create a successful real estate empire. (My mother is uncannily
> good with money, although still penurious.)

I remember never having any money and being told that although we lived in beautiful homes, this was only because these were my mother's investments. I was given an allowance contingent on fulfilling numerous chores. My allowance was five dollars a week and I think I got it twice between the ages of fourteen and eighteen. My mother was adamant that I earn everything I wanted. It took me two years to save up for a bicycle. I was one of the only kids in my high school not to have a car. I didn't have one until I was twenty-two; because all my friends were given cars, it never occurred to me to save for one.

We often ate at Howard Johnson, but from time to time we would go on trips and stay at the best hotels. When I visited my father, I never had any money. This would enrage my stepmother, who was furious that my mother got so much of my father's money. So, my father began slipping money to me on the side, a tradition that lasted until he died.

As we've seen, across class lines most young people grow up experiencing their situation as the norm. It often takes many years for us to question the myths our parents create. So it was for Victoria:

Until I was in my twenties, I believed that my father was well-off, but not as rich as many actors, which was more or less true; and that my mother didn't have a lot of money. When I was about seventeen [my mother] decided to buy herself a Mercedes. [She] hated to drive and I genuinely believed that she bought the car not for the status but because it felt like a tank and helped to calm her panic. But she was worried about what my father might think. So, she thought she would prepare him slowly by telling him that she had gotten a new car, but that she would surprise him with what kind when she next saw him. One day my father and I were driving and he asked: "So, your mother's gotten a new car? What kind?" And I, terrified of betraying my mother's secret, said that I didn't know what kind. My father looked at me as though I had completely lost my mind. I have always been a car nut and he absolutely knew that I knew what kind but simply wouldn't say.

As in so many families, money secrets were the glue that held relationships together:

I suppose [my father] thought my mother and I were just being idio-
syncratic, but really my mother and therefore I were always
worried about my father's disapproval of her use of her own money.
A general attitude of secrecy about money pervaded our family. I
never knew anything about any of my family's financial status
until three or so years ago.

My stepmother, a woman of extravagant tastes, bitterly
complained to anyone who would listen, throughout her marriage
to my father, that he did not support her in the style to which she
was accustomed. Her favorite gripe was that she even had to buy
her underwear with her own money. When she died, we all, including my father, discovered that she had two and a half million
dollars hidden away in tax-free accounts. She left it all to charity,
with a stipulation that my father should receive the interest for as
long as he lived. After she died, for the two-and-a-half years of his
illness, he often said that his sole goal in remaining alive was to get
as much of that money as he possibly could.

These money fears of the rich did not begin in the generation to which
Victoria's father and mother belonged. They had their origin long before,
in a family that knew wealth but was subject to the extremes of a market
economy:

My paternal great-grandfather was a successful inventor who
became a very wealthy man. But he lost his shirt in the crash of
1893. A terror of dying penniless loomed large over each of his
descendants. My father was no exception. The family money was
always handled by business managers and my father was very paranoid about losing money, and therefore very conservative. [He] was
critical of any money my mother ever spent, although he inevitably
appreciated the results, as she is an extremely talented and innovative designer who can make a little money go a very long way.

Inherited fears and the consequent nurturing of certain ideas and practices generated attitudes Victoria deals with today:

Our family certainly believed in the Protestant work ethic. Even
now, my mother will mutter "Get a job" under her breath if a
homeless person asks for money. But if a homeless person is playing the violin on the sidewalk, she considers that he or she is trying

to do something productive and she will give money. My mother doesn't give to people-related charities, only to organizations that save animals or maybe trees. My father gave and worked for charity, but only so far. At some point, he felt enough was enough. In fairness to him, half of his fan mail were requests for money from people who had an infinite number of misfortunes befall them, and I think he became a bit jaded.

Now in her thirties, Victoria understands how her life has been marked by the ways in which her family handled its money and her relationship to it. She observes that because she

never had access to the money by which I was surrounded, my whole life became geared toward getting money, although on some level I always carried with me that attitude that it was my due and therefore never made great sacrifices to get it. Throughout my early twenties I was constantly in financial and therefore emotional turmoil. My parents did not help, and often they criticized me. When I was twenty-six I declared bankruptcy. That changed my life. In court they gave us a big spiel about bankruptcy being a second chance, and I bought it. Since that time I have become responsible about money and have been well off. However, it's a bit like being a reformed addict of any kind. I have been able, more or less, to arrest or moderate my behavior, but the impulses are still there. I am compulsively generous with others and with myself. Even now, when I am depressed I go shopping and it gives me as much pleasure to buy or to do something for someone else as for myself. I have paid off every debt to friends that I incurred prior to my bankruptcy. More than one person told me that I was the only person who ever paid them back. I have lent countless people money. No one has ever paid me back. Since my father's death I have become both more cautious and more extravagant. In short, every day I am aware of my relationship to money, which exists on a continuum between a waltz and a battle.

It's not only the struggle Victoria herself must continue to wage with money, but how others relate to her in this regard. Whether she is in a period of financial stability or one of overspent terror, people always assume that she is rich. This is true in the sense that she has the security many lack. But it does not reflect the way she generally *feels* about herself, and the automatic assumption is not helpful to her ability to function well, nor does it ease her relationships with others:

> This has been a problem in friendships and relationships. In most cases I have been with people who made more money than I have. Often however, despite this, an inequity has existed along the lines of what I can only conclude is class. I have often been with people who were ill at ease with themselves in contrast to me, because of their perception of my background—movie star father, Ivy League education, knowledge of art, extensive travel, etc. Even when this has not been equated with money, it is an image that derives from money, for all these things are, to some degree, what money can buy.
>
> In my important relationships, there has always been a great deal of fluidity, of give and take with money. The attitude has generally been that the person who has the most money at the time can cover the other person and that that goes back and forth. I have generally been with people who did not feel possessive about their money but rather felt that money is a means to an end. However, since my father's death, although my financial situation has not drastically changed, I do have a cushion that I did not have and I have begun to realize that this has altered people's attitudes toward me. They think "She's set." I, on the other hand, live in constant fear that I am going to screw up and I'll wake up one morning and there will be nothing left.

In spite of her developing grasp of her financial situation, Victoria says that she is probably less conscious of her class and culture's attitude toward money than she is of other people's attitudes towards her perceived class and culture. She says these attitudes have ranged from obsequiousness to disdain, usually without attempting to discover what lies beneath her own agenda, practices, or fears. She remembers a particularly dramatic incident with a woman who was her lover for a time:

> When I lived with this woman, I remember showing her my parents' cookbook which contains pictures of our opulent house. She burst into tears, which was relatively uncharacteristic; and when I asked why, she told me that she'd "always hated the rich."

Some of the women to whom I sent questionnaires during the process of writing this book shared theirs with friends or sent copies on to other women whose stories they believed might interest me. Consequently, I received some answers with no name attached. Here are excerpts from one such anonymous response. It is clear it is a woman with money who speaks. Again, control is the leit motif of the woman/money relationship.

> [As a child] I felt privileged and self-defined a bit by my father's money. He handled it and we were affluent. The amount we had was never discussed. Poppa felt it was not important for the children to know the details. I do not know how much Mother knew. I do know she greatly resented having to ask my father for approval to buy things. Not that he wasn't quite generous in that regard, which he was, but I believe that she wanted control which she definitely did not have. She made a big point that I should never have to be dependent upon a man for my financial well-being.
>
> I am sure my Poppa felt that money was a status symbol. He had it while he grew up and all during his adult life. His life was privileged. He had a convertible Packard in his twenties, married a beauty queen, went to an Ivy League school, and was very successful in his business endeavors. We traveled a lot and by the time I was twenty-three I had been around the world three times and had gone on nine or ten luxury cruises.

This woman took her mother's admonition seriously, and it would shape her life:

> When I graduated from college, I began to support myself and no longer received help from home. Poppa died and I went to grad school. Tuition was paid through the trust that he set up in his will. After that, I was on my own. This was a huge adjustment.
>
> When I got married, money got tighter. Both travelers at heart, we continued to afford to see the unknown by living there, and we have spent five years abroad. But it took me a long time to get used to not having the same life style as before. It was a way of life, a routine. It was the style to which I had become accustomed. And I had to change.
>
> We returned to the States last year and I set up an office. I shop at WalMart. We rarely eat out. And I am very careful about what I spend for clothes. I have two kids and lots of love. I am happy . . .

but changing was hard. It was so hard that I bend over backwards not to let the kids know we have any money or that we'll inherit some. We drive modest cars. Both of us work (for ourselves) and the children see us work hard. I guess I am trying to cushion them from having to go through the change as I had to. My husband disagrees and it can be the source of some conflict.

I feel very lucky that my mother pushed me to earn my own way. I feel the control which I know she yearned for. Now, as a trustee for Poppa's trusts, she is in control and no one can tell her what she should do. So I suppose that my generation has disproved the myth that women should just be pretty as they have no head for numbers.

I am a consultant with many women as clients. I am just beginning to admit and see that they prefer to talk to me because I am a woman. They have been made to feel uneasy by my male colleagues. My mother has mentioned this feeling a lot and resents it terribly.

Having money in relation to others who do not may produce discomfort around such issues as loaning. While working people may easily hand one another a ten- or twenty-dollar bill—expecting or not that it will be repaid—when there is a marked difference in class the gesture may not be so easy. Jana, the wealthy photographer, tells the following anecdote:

> [In] a recent conversation I had with [my ex-husband] I was talking about loaning money to a friend because why is it fair that my father had money and hers didn't? That's why I think I should lend people money when they ask me. [He said] "the only thing wrong with what you've just said is father. Remember, the money came from your mother."
>
> It's a common way of thinking, that the man has made the money. Of course, my mother never worked a day in her life to earn money, and my father definitely enhanced her funds in his work life. But the money did come from her.

"Lend money, lose a friend" is a warning that is sadly often true; not because there is anything intrinsically wrong with helping a friend in need—quite the opposite in the American way—but because of how we have come to think and feel about money. Still, my respondents' stories indicate female creativity and rejection of this stereotype, pointing to the fact that healthier attitudes can indeed give birth to another, healthier, way of living.

Ruth, a feminist biologist in her early seventies, has managed to develop as healthy an attitude towards money as any I've come across. She has this to say about lending:

> I agree with my parents' sense that you should spend your money to do the things you need and, if possible, some of the things you want even though you don't need them. But accumulating it is for the birds. I give quite a bit to friends and organizations and would gladly give more if there weren't the stupid insecurity about the future. I have occasionally "lent" money, but never at interest unless people wanted to pay a minimal interest for their own reasons; and I don't expect to see much of the money I have "lent." It's mostly that some people feel better calling it that.

Ruth came to this country at the age of 14 when her Jewish socialist family fled the Nazi takeover of Austria. Having money certainly facilitated their escape, but money alone could not save them; it was only relative. Her family story of immigration holds clues to the money attitudes she later developed, including the way she feels about lending:

> At the point at which we left Vienna, four months after the Nazis took over, my parents were comfortable but not rich. We didn't own a car and rented the apartment in which we lived as well as the house we went to during summer vacations. But they did have money in the bank. My understanding is that, since we were not permitted to take any money with us, but could take goods, my parents bought some jewelry which they smuggled out. They also shipped all their furniture and medical office equipment and we all got clothes to last as long as possible. (My parents at their deaths— 30 and 50 years later—still had clothes they had bought in Vienna in 1938.) What money was left they gave to a gentile Austrian friend with directions to give to any of my parents' friends and relatives and anyone else who needed it in order to get out of Austria. We lived during the first year of our emigration on $2,000 my father managed to borrow from friends in Italy and Switzerland on our way to the United States.

Generation or age logically modified some of the responses I received from women with money. Younger women have had less time to reflect upon the issues. Renee is a college student in her early twenties. Her self-knowledge and attitudes are as much a result of coming to age in the Reagan–Bush years as they are of her relationship to inherited wealth. She writes:

> I always knew we had money, after all I grew up in the '80s where spending was in and Milken had not gotten caught yet. My brother and sister went away to college, got new cars when they turned 17, and I fully expected the same when it was my turn. I never knew and still don't know how much my dad actually made back then, had no idea how much money we needed to live very well, or to support five cars, two houses, a live-in housekeeper, a company plane, and the various vacations we took, summer sleep-away camp and ordinary living expenses.

Being the youngest among her siblings has also affected Renee's position and status:

> Most of my friends were the baby, like me, and so we could benefit even more from our parents' good fortune. I grew up in an upper-middle class suburb in New Jersey. In high school everyone was pretty much the same. Some kids got brand new cars when they were 17, some drove their parents' old BMW and Mercedes. Most of my friends had both parents still married, some had second homes in Florida and siblings in colleges away from home.
>
> I grew up with more televisions than I could count, my own telephone line, piano lessons, and we had an IBM computer that I started using when they first were adapted into the home. We had a second home in California . . . to me this was all normal, and I accepted it as such. Having money is a part of me. I know and wear expensive clothing, can identify and recognize name brands, had never set foot in a K-Mart until I was fifteen and I bought a fan in one.
>
> I never really became aware of how having money has marked my life until I came to college. My school is full of wealthy kids like myself who wear nice clothing and drive Saabs. But I found myself becoming friends with the kids who receive financial aid, those who have to work two jobs to be able to go out on weekends,

kids who are not on the full meal plan, who pay their own credit card bills, and some who never even had credit cards while I have three. I started to feel ashamed of my wealth.

For Renee, this recognition of "me and them" comes from beginning to know people different from herself, and also from some of what her college education has taught her. Her interpretation includes a dependence on so-called "reverse discrimination," not unlike the white person who riles against the anger of people of color and cannot internalize the fact that the discomfort of those with power cannot be likened to the privations suffered by those without:

> We often talk about classism and discrimination against poor students. But what people don't realize is that it can work both ways. I was embarrassed to bring my fancy red sports car back to school because of what people would think. I don't flaunt my money. I have nice things but I am very self-conscious of everything because of the way I was brought up.
>
> I always have a lot of cash on me and lend my friends money whenever they need it. One thing that sticks in my mind is freshman year coming home from Christmas break. My parents use a car service that picks us up from the airport. I needed to be picked up at school and so my parents sent a driver to come and get me in my own car so I could drive home. Part of me was appalled; I would have loved it if my parents could have come up and taken me home. I was embarrassed telling people how I was going to get there . . . it was weird.

She admits:

> In relationships the issue of money is a tough one. Since I am not creative, I tend to buy things for people I care about. This can create an unequal dynamic in which there is an awful lot of resentment and anger.
>
> Sometimes I try to hide the fact that I have money because I don't want people judging me accordingly. I dress nicely most of the time, but then again I like to walk around and be comfortable and my mother feels that I embarrass myself and by association her. Then sometimes I try to hide behind my wealth because that is all that I know. It is my life.

Such is the dis-ease of a young woman whose family money sets her apart. Whether or not she becomes a Sallie Bingham or a Genevieve Vaughan, or even just gets comfortable with her own monied place in the world, will depend upon a combination of factors. Ours is a society in which patriarchy and capitalism conspire to an ever greater refinement of double-speak. Information, statistics, even values and options are less and less what they seem. Language is bereft of meaning. Meaning itself loses meaning. The myth becomes the metaphor.

I call it "Gumping" our collective consciousness, after *Forrest Gump*, the popular 1994 film whose protagonist of the same name is a mildly retarded or intellectually slow white male who manages nonetheless to live a charmed life. His story touches on a range of issues: everything from the big ones like race, class, and gender, to the historically- and geographically-situated events that showcase these so dramatically: making it as someone different through the U.S. public education system, the Vietnam War and the movement against it, AIDS, and the integrity of American presidents. Gump solves all problems and becomes a lovable success without really addressing any of the complex contradictions.

Forrest Gump is immensely likeable. Funny too. He moves through life as if charmed, saving his buddies in battle and standing up to authority. A strong and loving mother, an uncomplicated and congenial small southern town, the enduring friendship (or is it sympathy?) of a school chum, as well as indomitable loyalty, perseverance, and luck, bring him to unimagined pinnacles of success. Gump's message is that the well-meaning can win, even if they aren't that smart. Keep plodding along. Stick up for your friends. Issues such as race and class and physical or mental difference won't get in the way if you pretend them away.

The culture of denial.

Today's political and social rhetoric reflects the Gumpian ethic. It enables us to perceive the invasion of Haiti as if it were a friendly restoration of democracy; to accept the nightly news reports from Bosnia without asking why they don't make sense; to believe that the economy is "growing" even as we and our friends lose jobs—"economic crisis is as economic crisis does";[16] to express national relief that universal health care reform is no longer on the legislative agenda, although great numbers of Americans lack access to adequate medical attention; to be seduced by the pizza commercial and then seduced by the commercial immediately following, that offers the "secret" of weight loss. In short, to accept and reproduce the double-speak and double-act of a system that uses us as pawns.

This conditioning, constant and subliminal, makes it easier for us to ignore the contradiction between the feminization of poverty on the one hand and the great number of wealthy women on the other. Women with money are not accustomed to thinking of themselves as powerful because they have specifically been taught to abdicate power. A tradeoff for what we are told is happiness?

Arrogance, guilt, shame, and isolation take the place of generosity of spirit, practicality, wisdom, and community. This particularly North American conditioning manipulates rather than guides, abuses rather than teaches creative use. And it keeps many of us complacent when told that "women don't have a head for figures."

Change is dialectical. Women's struggles for greater educational and workplace equity have broadened and deepened to philosophical questions that are no longer limited by notions of equality alone. Feminism challenges traditional moralities, and the consequent creative social change provides arenas in which women, and men, may exercise our potential. Only the realization of this potential will make it possible for us to emerge alive from the death-dealing limitations that have been imposed upon us, and that we consequently impose upon ourselves.

How We Change

6

or Some Alternatives to Money as Power

What rivets me to history is seeing
acts of survival turned
to rituals of self-hatred. This
is colonization. . .
—Adrienne Rich

Suppose I were hit by a Mack truck tomorrow; how
would my checkbook stubs reflect what I care about?
—Gloria Steinem

The frequency and widespread nature of gendered money inequity as
well as the use of money to manipulate women's lives hasn't only
produced a general craziness about the subject. It has also pushed us to
seek alternative ways of thinking about economics; and alternative
designs for saving, spending, and joining our financial lives to men—or to
other women. Perhaps because the old forms have been far less beneficial
to women than to men, we seem to be looking for new forms more
creatively and more of us seem to be engaged in the search.

In spite of the conservative backlash, notions of gender equity perme-
ate our society today. They have been absorbed into our expectations
and assumptions. Younger women have benefited from feminism and
tend to be much more independent. Older feminists and lesbian feminists want to understand the money knowledge often denied us as we
grew up. More women today than at any previous time choose to live

independently, sometimes even when romantically involved with a man or another woman. And women who live with their partners are more adventurous, more creative, less likely to follow unhealthy patterns of money management.

Our biggest struggle seems to be against the forms, both crude and subtle, that money manipulation may take in our lives. As we begin to recognize how we are used, how we in turn use others, and how this use damages our relationships, many of us try to divest ourselves of practices we paid little attention to before. A general validation of feelings as well as of "pure reason" has helped make us aware of much of the distortion. Speaking directly, rather than crawling around the issue, is an important first step.

Challenge takes many shapes, and there are all sorts of arrangements. A number of women who responded to my questionnaire keep their monies entirely separate, believing that this is necessary to maintaining their sense of independence. Others see a lack of trust in separateness; they feel that only by merging completely can they fully commit or achieve relational harmony. Still others have a household account for common expenses, while retaining a personal account where they can exercise some freedom of individual expression.

Creative financial arrangements are common, and among my narrators there were almost as many of these as there were stories. Class background, culture, attitudes in family of origin, generation, or age, whether or not dependant children are involved, and many other factors affect decisions about merging money or keeping it apart.

In spite of the fact that society continues to push dependency of many sorts, independence—however each of us may define it—has become a positive value for women. It is true that we are bombarded with messages suggesting that reliance upon a man, the latest fashion statement, a particular body size and shape, or an ideology which would seem to place us at the top of whatever pyramid, will bring success. The current conservative backlash encourages and rewards this system of values. So women as a group, and groups of women, may move backwards and then take positive leaps in our search for ourselves. The forward motion may not always be steady, but it *is* a forward motion. And despite the current trend towards values oppressive to women, the gains we've made will not be easily erased. Independence has become a household word with regard to the pursuit of personal goals within a relationship, decisions concerning work, domestic and childrearing responsibilities, personal space, and the management of money.

Women's quest for financial independence came through in answers given by those from supportive backgrounds as well as by those who had been maneuvered, exploited, or oppressed as children. Hannah is a Jewish heterosexual divorced mother of one, in her late sixties, and now retired from her career as an art history professor. Her family lived through and was economically shaped by the depression, yet her parents managed to give her a sense of stability and security. She voices a long-term reluctance to depend financially upon a domestic partner:

> I am now 68, retired from teaching with what I hope will be an adequate pension in the future of our globe, with sufficient savings in the bank from years of living frugally to meet my needs. . . . My only son (now married) is a close friend. We were a family of two, with brief ventures into unsatisfactory marriages and many lovers who had to respect my independence by not tendering any money (which a few had with surplus) toward anything but buying dinner and theater tickets. I would not permit any contribution toward living expenses or child care because I did not allow them to live in my house.

In Jewish immigrant families, even when these remained working class, parents usually saw to it that culture was accessible and the mothers especially proved inventive in terms of making it available, as well as innovative with regard to general living conditions. Hannah is the daughter of such a family.

> My mother handled the money my father earned as a waiter. Her policy was to never burden us (my sister and I) with worries, financial or other[wise]. I got my culture in New York's museums, libraries, and even concert halls where for $1.00 we could stand in the back of Carnegie Hall or the Met (until we sneaked to empty seats after the first intermission). We got dance classes and other cultural training in centers established in various parts of the city. [Mother] found money for an old piano, and for piano lessons, though we lived in three rooms. As a seamstress, she hid our poverty with curtains, clothing (the fur collar on the cloth coat,

the homemade prom evening dress with a borrowed velvet cloak
. . .). We were definitely "different": poor, immigrants with accents
(my parents), my lack of certain English words until I was a
teenager though born in the U.S., being Jewish, and being female in
a culture that wanted intellectual achievement—from the boys.

So often class is hidden. We are who we are, and as children that is
what we know. We see ourselves as average, ordinary, "like everyone
else." Or, we may feel different but not understand why. Race and
culture are more obvious. But the way they determine money attitudes is
always strongly provoked by the ways in which all the variables intersect, and an immigrant childhood or growing up with first generation
immigrant parents can be central. In this family difficult economic
circumstances were faced with honesty and courage. A strong bent
towards independence stayed with Hannah as a result.

Judith is the activist and older returning student in her mid-forties
whose family of origin was at the poor end of an extended lower-middle-
class clan. Her parents were manipulative where money was concerned,
frequently making her feel that she cost too much. Hers was a troubled
childhood. Her need to maintain economic independence is every bit as
serious as Hannah's; but her money and possessions are like friends who
may comfort or betray:

> I would never, ever co-mingle my money with anyone else's. Of all
> the people I have lived with, I have been lucky in that none of
> them has ever swindled me. I am very careful that anyone I deal
> with financially pays their share. My apartment has been robbed
> twice and it felt like I lost a loved one. A former friend once took
> an old computer I bought and some money I gave him with the
> understanding that he would upgrade it for me at cost. He never
> returned it or my money or attempted to make restitution.
> Nothing that has ever happened to me in my life has made me as
> upset and angry as that.

I found that women make qualitative changes in their lives more
easily when they are able to assess their current situation, remember
what messages they internalized growing up, and then act upon an
understanding of the ways in which their behavior continues to draw

upon that early conditioning. Male socialization and its resultant attitudes are also necessarily a part of the picture. But it is the woman who more often demands change.

Grace, the TV producer whose childhood you may remember included a particularly controlling father, describes money in her marriage in vivid detail:

> My husband comes from a great deal of money. He is, his personality is, almost a reaction to it. When we were first together, I had just gotten out of debt. We kept separate accounts. I moved into his apartment, and later into the apartment he'd purchased before we met. It was considerably more expensive than my own. He lived more extravagantly than I. I resented that my expenses increased when I moved in with him. I'd lived on such a strict budget for so long that I seethed at him when he asked me to pay "my half of the rent." I also hated relinquishing control. . . . It felt like a divisive thing. I didn't mind paying the rent (though only his name was on the lease, and later on the mortgage); I hated paying *him*. He became my landlord. It was a power play I couldn't live with.
>
> Then I realized it was *his* divisive thing too. It kept distance between us at a time when that was important for him. He was protecting himself from me. And so, as I committed to the relationship, I forced him to merge our funds. It was a fight at first, but it works so much better now for both of us. We keep separate credit accounts. We each treat ourselves to big purchases without consulting one another. We also both have veto power on them. We have our respective nest eggs, but I kick into our account when we need it, and so does he.

Grace is 16 years younger than her husband, and, as she explains, he also came into the marriage with much more money. She says her one holdout with the above arrangement is that she's still terrified to take time off from her high-powered job to have a family. She hasn't been able to imagine not working hard to earn her share of their combined income. Grace adds that she "guess[es] that means I learned not to value my mother's work when she was a full-time mother." I wonder if she might not also retain feelings of money inadequacy; if her husband provided their entire income for a while, wouldn't that create a further power imbalance?

This is particularly interesting in light of a story Grace tells about her parents' relationship. In her childhood, money truly became a vehicle for revenge:

> My father inherited a great deal of money from his father. He was warned, however, that he would get nothing if he left my mother in advance of my grandfather's death. My father left my mother after the will was executed. He took advantage of my mother's love for him and gave her very little . . . promising he'd remarry her some-day if she didn't challenge his settlement. [Then] he ran off with a younger woman. He squandered his money. She invested hers. One day she had more than he did. This was just about the time he quit drinking and left the younger woman.
>
> My mother was desperately in love with him still. But now she had [the] power—money. She refused to remarry him, opting instead for living with him. She shared with him. She forced him to share with her. She struck deals. She wanted to run a soup kitchen/ministry. She needed a building. My father's end of the deal was to create a space for that. He fixed up a building, according to her needs. They built a much stronger marriage out of wedlock. Eventually she married him again. On her terms.

Some of my narrators experienced the discomfort and confusion of money manipulation for years, and have a hard time extricating themselves from the tensions. Bernarda, the Mexican American journalist and writer in her forties whose upper-middle-class parents had an explosive relationship around issues of money management, fears she reproduces their tug of war with her own partner. "The greatest struggle I'm having now," she says, "is how I deal with money vis-à-vis my husband.

> I'm the primary breadwinner. He's a freelance photographer, some-one whose talent I wanted to nurture when we fell in love. . . . We keep separate checking accounts. I pay rent, food, and utilities. He covers his photo supplies. What is horrible is that there are times when I'll throw this in his face if I'm angry about something else. I used to pick fights almost subconsciously whenever I'd pay the bill, just like Dad . . . after some of our fights I'd wonder if I wasn't punishing myself for "costing my parents money" as a kid, by marrying someone I am supporting.

Marjorie's marriage included a veritable litany of money madness. The communications expert and mediator in her fifties, her finances have gone up and down and then up again. She is now a respected professional living in semi-poverty but with a teaching opportunity on the horizon. She remembers money in her family of origin as the proverbial "secret topic." She says she

> fluctuates . . . in the ease with which I deal with money in primary relationships. The man I married and I had a single account, until he withdrew most of that money and went off to spend a month with his girlfriend in New Zealand, leaving me with no knowledge of what he had done until the rent check bounced.

They had separate accounts after that.

Marjorie remembers her marriage as one in which both partners talked about one being the primary breadwinner while the other pursued his ideals; but how it was she who most often worked while he enjoyed a greater freedom. Patriarchal social attitudes, however, forced her to evolve an unusual financial relationship with this husband who eventually became her ex.

> Fifteen years ago, when I first separated . . . I couldn't find anyone who would rent to me without my husband's signature and guarantee. He gave it, but the landlord wouldn't even do a repair unless my husband requested it. [My ex-husband] is paying my rent again now, but my current landlords always call me about everything— including late rent checks (though they know my situation).

Societal attitudes as well as a collective history of patriarchal obstacles can stand in the way of healthier money management. It is always hard to opt for a different choice. Jeannette, the working-class woman who is trying to write full time, addresses money and worth, which brings up guilt, and also the issue of class. Economically supported by her husband, she still insists on the proverbial account of her own.

> By far the biggest troubles [my husband] and I have had have been around the issue of money. He comes from a somewhat more stable, middle-class family than I, and I understand that his family associates poverty with unworthiness. [We] have had some long

protracted discussions on this subject, and he's come a long way, baby, but there is also in him an easiness about money, the confidence that he can get [what] he needs, that he'll never be destitute ... [so] he's not as conservative as I am in spending. I can't stand debt [and we've] incurred more than I'm comfortable with.

Money is complicated for us, too, because he is supporting me while I write. This induces guilt on my part, and I often feel a need to earn some money of my own, either by taking a temporary secretarial job or [whatever]. More and more I feel that I must make a paying career of this or else find a [real] job.

[My husband] gives me a fixed amount from which to run the household (he used to pay the bills until it made me too crazy—he was too lax about it), and we'd sometimes get shut-off notices on the utilities, simply because he'd forgotten or not gotten around to paying. I'm compulsive about paying the bills on time, and thus I'm much more comfortable when I have control of that. We have separate credit cards and separate bank accounts, though our money is almost entirely *his,* or has been earned by him. I could not stand to have a joint account with him (or anyone, I think) because I need the control of knowing absolutely what I have.

Racial and cultural considerations may also come into play. Maylene is black and in her early fifties. She grew up one of ten siblings in a town of sugarcane cutters in the deep south. Both parents and each child as he or she was old enough to work supported the family by picking beans and every one of the children went through college—a history replete with the sort of determination, effort, and faith that cannot be imagined by most of the country's amorphous "middle class."

Maylene earned a Master's degree in Education, worked as a school teacher, assistant principal, and principal, and was recently elected to the City Council of a Florida beach town. Still, her history of childhood hardship, a family tradition of hard work and tenacity, and a culture that urges women to stick by their men conspired in delaying her recognition that she was being held back by an irresponsible husband. Not long ago she divorced her spouse of 29 years and she says that at least one of the reasons was money based:

At first it was easy [to deal with money in the relationship]. Later it became a problem for him [and] he became a problem for me. There never was money. In the future it will be mine and ours. Love will have nothing to do with it, nor *color*.

Maylene has this to say about women and money in the relationships she's experienced or seen:

> It *has* changed. Some of the women of my generation who has moved up the ladder has chosen to stay away from a serious relationship—our black brothers has problems dealing with the strong financially secure black women. I feel after 50 you do need an escort, [but] with aid, nothing else.

Sonia is a Mexican American writer in her early forties. She recently remarried, and has an eleven-year-old son from a previous relationship. When Sonia was a child, her family was "poor working class." Her mother was an orphan who at the age of 11 began working as a maid in her native Mexico City, and she continued as a factory worker to be the family's main support until Sonia was ten. Her father eventually found steady work, but "kept what he did not contribute to the household expenses for himself to do as he pleased." Sonia's grandmother's relief checks were used for monthly groceries: "big sacks of white flour for tortillas . . . frijoles, rice, greens, coffee."

> I never forgot hunger as a child, anemia, decalcinated teeth, underweight, flour-sack underslips, boys' Maxwell St. irregular socks, huge rodents and armies of cockroaches. My older sister seems to remember a time when I was so sickly at about six or seven that she thought I was going to die. When we were relocated by the city because of urban renewal and our flat was a bit improved, we lived for ten years under the tyrannous racism of Italian landlords.

Given these origins, Sonia's feelings about sharing money with her husband are understandably cautious:

> [We've] been together over a year now and we do keep finances somewhat separate, with separate checking accounts. Because of being a writer my income varies sometimes greatly from year to year. We are working it out and plan to open a joint account next year for our shared living expenses. Yes, trust and early history do

play a big part on how two adults bring their hard-earned dollars together. Also, I bring a minor into the partnership which complicates things.

And she adds:

> Love and money are sometimes synonymous for me. Because I feel that I was neglected materially growing up I equate gifts from a lover with the value the lover has placed on me. I know this is antithetical to my usual independent, feminist, confident persona. I'm not proud of it but I'm not ashamed to ask it either because I am trying to heal a very old wound by pampering the child in me who was shamefully neglected.
>
> In my partnership it has changed because we discuss our money matters openly and we are both steady income earners. What will change for my son is that he will not be expected to help me out after high school and I will be prepared to support his pursuit of higher education if he chooses it.

Women inherit the curse of dependency, and this is manifest not only when a husband, father, boss, or male friend assumes control of the finances. We are inundated by social expectations about money management. Demeaning or oppressive assumptions form the backdrop to our entire social interaction. Rachel, the musician and faculty grants officer whose mother convinced her dying father's company to keep him on the payroll, describes how money became the last battleground in her own marriage and divorce. When everything else was finished, it remained the source of multiple frustrations:

> As my marriage dissolved, the question of money was of prime importance. I wanted to salvage as much as possible for myself and the kids, and obviously so did my husband. [Money] was the only link between us and the only area in which we could focus our anger, desire for revenge, and fear of impoverishment.

Rachel admits that "one of the prime reasons for staying in my bad marriage was fear of poverty." And she offers an anecdote that is all too common in the context of bourgeois psychotherapy:

A family psychologist we saw several weeks after separation suggested to me that I might find it financially unfeasible to get a divorce and to "make it on my own." I responded that to go back for that reason alone was as close to prostitution as anything I could fathom.

Heterosexual women, to one degree or another, often remain imprisoned by the conditioning that requires they "ask permission" of a man. The fact that we may choose to make our lives with another women, however, doesn't automatically signal the desire or capacity for alternative money management. Whatever our sexual identity, we are products of the same patriarchal system and tend to reedit its abuses in our primary relationships. But lesbian couples, perhaps because they are forced by a heterosexist society to examine more closely their living arrangements, often come up with more innovative plans.

In looking at the financial arrangements of women who share their lives with other women, it's important to understand that joining finances holds a different meaning for them than for heterosexuals. For one thing, in most cases the worker or professional with benefits cannot extend her health policy to cover her partner; that fact alone may slice a couple of hundred dollars a month off a middle-class family income—much more if there are large medical expenses.

Two women may feel they must keep that extra bedroom around for the benefit of uncomprehending relatives. In an emergency, a living or regular will may be contested. Taxes cannot be filed jointly. And women living alone, lesbian or not, are more vulnerable in our society; therefore we may feel we need a more secure (i.e., expensive) environment—a "better" neighborhood, an apartment within protected space, or some other added expenditure. In these scenarios, emotional hardship for lesbians often becomes a logical outgrowth of, and indistinguishable from, financial stress.

When there is a marked difference in class background and/or earning potential between one woman and the other, additional money-related problems may be added to the core difficulties lesbians face. Two women tend to believe they are alike, that they can naturally sense one another's feelings and needs; then class rears its head and the problems surface. A couple who has been together for close to twenty years speaks movingly of struggles and solutions.

Sam is a working-class woman from an Italian family whose early years were marked not only by poverty issues but also by the fact that she never could or wanted to pass. She became a steel worker, one of very few women in a tough job traditionally held by men. Without a college education she earned a high salary for dangerous work. When the steel mills began laying people off, Sam was forced to look for another job. In a shrinking market and with few other salable skills, she eventually ended up repairing books in a library, earning much less than she had at the mill.

Sam's long-time partner, Wanda, is from a Jewish professional family in which she was raised to satisfy her intellectual curiosity, study at the best schools, and achieve the profession of her choice. Marriage was expected, but perhaps no more than education. She became an anthropologist and moved into a tenured university position. As a political activist (both women are), Wanda made the complex journey to full professorship and now makes considerably more than her lover.

Sam and Wanda taped a joint response to my questionnaire. This produced a fascinating text, for along with both women's reminiscences of very different childhoods and adolescent years, they got into a discussion about the money issues that continue to plague them after close to twenty years of life together. Here is the part of their conversation in which they discuss keeping their incomes separate:

> Sam: This is the first relationship that I've done that with. All my other relationships, each of us put, you know, our money went into the same account, and we'd draw from it. And it might be because the pay was more equal. You know, I make $30 thousand less a year than you, Wanda, so . . .

> Wanda: But we kept it separate when you and I were earning more or less the same, at the beginning. . . .

> Sam: Yeah, but that was because it was the beginning. I think if I were still earning the money I was earning at the steel plant, we would have it together since we bought the house.

> Wanda: Well, that's interesting. I'm not so sure that we would. Because, see, I kept everything together with [my husband] and I thought that was a mistake. Because I felt ripped off by him.

Sam: Well he never put anything into it. . . .

Wanda: Right. And so I had decided I was going to keep my account separate in the future. But I think also I felt I wanted to keep my account separate from you because I knew that we have such different attitudes towards money that we would get in trouble. Because you spend whatever you have plus three thousand more. And that would drive me bananas. I just couldn't deal with it. So this way we keep it completely separate, we don't snoop around in one another's handling of finances, and I don't have to complain too much about all the different things you buy and I can even enjoy them, sometimes. But I do think we could do better.

    No, wait, I also want to say something and I'll see whether you agree: that although it's completely separate, we also have a household account that we each pay into, a prorated amount, according to our income. So, like I pay in $525 a month and you pay in $300.

Sam and Wanda have honed their class and cultural differences over the years. They laugh a lot about the agreements they've reached, clearly workable ones for them, especially in the larger context of sharing monthly expenditures for the home they own, and for travel. Still, smaller contradictions remain. Wanda, who grew up with much more in the way of opportunity, saves more stringently. Working-class Sam buys more and enjoys frequent breakfasts and lunches out. Listen to them on the subject of restaurant eating. Wanda, still in the presence of Sam, begins to speak about, rather than to, her partner:

Wanda: You know, we run out of money at different times, since I'm not paid in the summer. I'm always out of money in August, and Sam is always there with a loan from her credit union for me. So those kinds of things aren't tense. What's tense for me are those ten and twenty dollars that pay for her lunch and breakfast, which I view as completely extravagant. I eat my breakfast home. I take my lunch. But because we have separate accounts, I don't say a word. Except in a joking manner. And like now . . .

Sam: (responds directly to Wanda) I don't have any trouble with the way we handle money. You help me out, I help you out ... and you know, you pay for most of the travel. I take care of any spending money that I might incur. But you usually pay the airfares. And our entertainment, like when we go to the theater; then I'll help pay for dinners. . . .

Wanda: Sometimes. If you have the money you always do. You're never cheap, if you have the money, about dinner. But I guess I would like you to think about us going out to dinner more.

Sam: Uhuh. I like to go to breakfast . . .

Wanda: Right. And I like to go to dinner, so . . .

These daily differences reflect opposing childhood realities, accounting for differing attitudes in our formative years. Wanda describes a father in absolute control of family finances: "It was his province, and I think he told us that," she remembers. He would frequently criticize her mother and accuse her of being a spendthrift. "As I look back on it," Wanda remembers, "I think it was the dignity with which she handled those interchanges that taught me something about fighting, or struggling, in different situations."

Wanda also tells a story that eloquently illustrates her father's pride in caring for his own. She won a scholarship to an expensive Ivy League college, and says: "My father turned it down because he felt that as a citizen it was his duty to send his daughter to college if he could."

Sam's family of origin was very different from Wanda's. She speaks of her mother as having been "very definitely in charge of the money." Her father was the sole breadwinner—when she was in grade school he told her once that he made $35 a week—but he would hand his check over to his wife and she managed all expenditures. They were always in debt:

It was never that they *didn't* have debt. Everything they bought they bought on some kind of credit. And I remember my mother wanted a brass lamp. You know, those salesmen used to come door to door, and they'd come weekly to get paid. And I remember her buying this pretty brass lamp that she always kept in her window. And my father never knew that it had payments on it. One time the guy came when he was there and she shooed him, you know,

she told him that he had the wrong door, and he was smart enough
to catch on. Everybody knew about the lamp but my father.

Sam also has a story that provides an interesting counterpoint to
Wanda's rejected scholarship. During the depression her father was
forced to go on welfare. But he never believed he'd had a right to simply
keep what the government had made available:

> Before he died he paid it all back again. It used to drive my mother
> crazy that he said he was working and he was earning money and
> the money needed to go to somebody else that needed it. He paid
> back every dime that he got during the depression.

Both these women's fathers worked hard and evidenced extreme pride
in being able to support their families. Both their mothers managed the
money with skill, although the working-class wife had more real control
over much less money. Putting away for education and savings was
possible in Wanda's family and became a primary value. In Sam's family
saving was impossible; there was barely enough to make it from day to
day. It's easy, then, to understand why having breakfast and lunch out is a
pleasure Sam is reluctant to give up and why Wanda yearns to save for
larger luxuries, worrying when she cannot.

A number of my lesbian narrators say that the moment they were able
to put economic dependency behind them and make a successful change
in the way they handled money coincided with their sexual coming out.
Again, the first isn't automatically linked to the second, but confronting
one issue does seem to deepen the courage needed to confront others.

Jessica, a retired administrative assistant in her mid-sixties, grew up in
a loving family she describes as "addicted to a religion that required
them to bring the 'truth' door-to-door to all types of people." She was
married for many years, then divorced and assumed her lesbian identity.
Her relationship with her woman partner is now also long term. Jessica
describes dealing with money throughout these two very different times
in her life:

> Money was a big problem in my 24-year marriage. Although my
> husband was the sole wage-earner and I was the stay-at-home
> mom, it was assumed that I would handle the family finances. But

it became a never-ending battle to deal with the nasty little surprises that would always turn up in the bank statement. Money to him was prestige and extravagant gifts meant love, and the luxuries he bought (in secret, lots of times) were mostly in the "dollar down, a dollar a month" category.

With this history, it is understandable that she searched for a different strategy:

> In my current 12-year relationship with my woman life-partner, we began with the understanding that our money would always be separate, and that we would never want to feel obliged to stay together because our finances were too intermingled to untangle. . . . I find it satisfying to know that I have no one to answer to in this area. It means security for me which was missing in my life with my free-spending husband, from whom I received nothing in community property after a 24-year marriage. [And it's] worked well, even in periods when our individual incomes were widely disparate, because it allows for each partner to practice her own money habits, however bizarre they may be, without having to be questioned or dissuaded.

As with Sam and Wanda, sometimes both members of a lesbian couple responded to my questionnaire. Betty and Barbara are in their sixties. Betty is from a working-class background; her father was a Swedish immigrant who worked as a janitor, and her mother also worked, as a bookkeeper. Barbara's childhood was more comfortable; her parents had an antique and gift shop. For many years these women have owned a bookshop together. Betty was a professor until she retired, and has this to say about their shared finances:

> I realize that I have been the primary wage earner in my relationships, all of them with women. I have not kept finances separate, but until fairly recently I have held property and checking accounts in my name. It never has worried me if a partner didn't bring money to a relationship. I guess I always managed to find someone who brought household skills like cooking—things I can't do. Without examining it, I put partners in the role of "housewife" to my "husband"—without extreme role playing.

Barbara, in her separate response, agrees that "our finances are not separate now and never have been. I have never been the primary financial earner in this partnership," she admits,

> but it's not always easy to deal with, because there is something embarrassing about asking if you run short. Only in the last few years have I had money enough of my own. Nonetheless, as a rule, household money is kept in a box from which we take whatever is needed for *any* cash transaction.

In the responses I gathered, women of vastly differing experiences speak about their choices and how they work, or don't. Particularly interesting are couples, homosexual and heterosexual, in which one partner earns or has inherited considerably more than the other. In such situations, and in a society in which money so clearly translates into power, it helps to develop a profound consciousness about how that power is wielded. Solutions have to be truly innovative and supportive of both partners to work.

Some couples have established a sliding scale in which each contributes a percentage based on what she or he earns. Some sequence time, alternating lifestyles with regard to income and expenditure. Some require lengthy processing procedures and frequent check-ins in which both partners try to overcome childhood trauma and deal honestly with their finances. Others avail themselves of techniques or attempt strategies that never do work and often end up damaging a relationship beyond repair. Money dysfunction is certainly as common as sexual or substance-abuse dysfunction, and ever so much less discussed.

Younger women today come up in a world with many more alternatives than those available to their mothers. They aren't as likely to accept a situation in which they are relegated to housekeepers for spouses who work, or any of the emotional variations on that theme. In fact, that time-honored tradition is no longer even the norm. Whether because more women demand their own profession or by virtue of an economic crisis that makes it necessary for more of them to work, few young women today see their future dependent upon a man's support.

Perception hasn't caught up with reality, though. Despite their changing expectations (and needs), today's young women remain bombarded with images that continue to picture them smiling up into the eyes of a protective father figure. And men continue to receive a similar image, from all but explicitly feminist women. So women starting out on the adventure of designing their primary relationships have some double messages to decode and work through. Several young women shared with me the ways in which they confront the challenge.

Dora is 27, a bilingual teacher in the public schools with plans for a graduate degree somewhere in her future. She is still struggling to combine meaningful work, her considerable political commitment, and her relationship with a young man. Dora's parents were political activists on the left, uninterested in material things. They were open and generous with their daughter:

> My parents always spent money on phone calls and plane trips for their kids, flying us to and from their home. They inherited money and went from being activists without a lot to being [activist] lawyers. They hardly ever go out to dinner or buy new clothes, and live on about $100 a week. My mother pays the bills and my father avoids thinking about money at all.
>
> They never wanted me to bypass important opportunities because of their cost. They've collectively been very generous. When I've asked for something, my father has said I should ask my mother. My mother tells me to talk to my father only about the idea of what I need money for, not so much to solicit approval of the amount [requested].
>
> As a young child I think I was pretty ignorant about money issues. [As I got older], when I have asked about their income, retirement plans, etc., they have been very straightforward with me. Money means more [to me] now, because I have experienced periods of not having enough, of being unemployed, of having to live more simply, or of having to borrow. I didn't learn "the value of money" until I had to support myself.

Dora admits that money issues have caused friction in her intimate relationships.

> One lover of three-and-a-half years and I split up partly because we made our money decisions in opposite ways. He always wanted to be "secure" and save for the future. I made decisions based on what

I wanted to do in the present, trusting that money would be there. I tried to conform to his way of doing things and felt very unhappy. [Now] I make about $12,000 to $13,000 a year. I'd rather have very little on a monthly or yearly basis but gain meaningful experiences.

In my current romantic relationship of two years I have mostly felt that I had more money than my partner, although this situation is changing. He is a radical musician. I've had more access to family money than he, and we have fallen back on that sometimes. Last year he went to teacher's college to become a bilingual elementary school teacher. I decided not to pay off his $20,000 student loan because we are not married. If we were married I would pay it off.

I have felt a lot of stress when both my lover and I have been out of work. And I have felt bad when I've had to use savings to pay for things for both of us. I feel my partner and I share a journey, [but] I would still be on this journey without him. We are waiting to decide about life-long or very long commitments, as we experiment to see whether we can truly accommodate each other's needs and goals.

Still, Dora sums up her and her partner's money philosophy by affirming: "We take risks. We are full human beings. Our economic freedom allows us more leverage in relationships and decisions about our lives."

Sondra is a young middle-class Jewish woman, a poet currently in graduate school and planning on becoming a teacher of literature. She is unusually articulate, both about the forces that influenced class and attitude in her family of origin and about the tensions between her parents that eventually led to their divorce.

I grew up in the traditional feminine mystique environment of the early 1970s. My dad worked (he's a college professor, with a Ph.D. in Physics) and my mom stayed home when we were young (she has a M.A. in English). Ours was a suburban home. My dad's parents were immigrants from Eastern Europe, who worked in minimum-wage jobs and saw money as something to be hoarded, not spent. My mom's family was more middle class, her parents were born in the U.S. and her father was an airline pilot.

My dad controlled the money, and had (still has, but to a much lesser degree) major hangups about finances. He is terribly afraid of debt, and when he and my mom bought a house, they bought one she didn't like. The one she favored would have required a loan from my mom's family, and my dad refused to ask. More interestingly, my mom didn't feel as though as a woman she was in a position to ask her parents.

In many ways, my dad was stingy with money. Though I never lacked what I needed, and certain things like education were more valued than other things, the spirit in which he gave lacked generosity. He didn't know how to enjoy money. For instance, when he was a child, his parents didn't celebrate birthdays, so he didn't understand why it was so important to my mom to do so. Years of therapy have helped my dad with his hangups, but when I was young and we were a one-income family, money was a major issue.

Sondra considers her background upper-middle class. She reflects on her family history and its impact on her own attitudes:

I think that the way in which my parents spent money has marked me more than the amount of money I've had or not had. I work hard at enjoying money and figuring out what my priorities are. For instance, having my own space has been important, so ... I am reluctant to share an apartment even though I would have more money to spend on other things. When I was a child we didn't go out to eat that often, so I feel guilty sometimes when I eat outside my home—if it's not necessary or a special occasion. I also make conscious efforts to use money to give other people pleasure, and will buy trinkets or little gifts that I know my friends or lovers will like. I worried for a long time that people might think I'm cheap, the way I used to feel about my dad.

What her father might think about her lifestyle, how he might judge it, is still a concern for Sondra:

I'm becoming seriously involved with a man right now who has accumulated a great deal of student loans. While this doesn't bother me, I won't tell my father, who fears debt, because I don't want to worry him or have him misperceive my boyfriend as irresponsible with money, or as using me to help pay back his loans.

Pondering these young women's dilemmas and strategies for change inevitably points us back to our mothers, and makes us more conscious of the ways some of them have tried to provide their children with alternatives to the conventional money assumptions (or failed to do so). Mothers' patterns, in turn, reflect their own childhood experiences. One generation builds on the lessons of the one before, of course, but my explorations suggest that qualitative change must be supported by conscious choice.

Phoebe is an historian in her forties. She is white, the mother of a son, married, divorced, and recently remarried. She begins her response to my questionnaire, as did a number of my other narrators, by revealing that she "[has] not looked forward to this task. I have known that writing answers to your questions will uncover pain that, up until now, I have managed by ignoring." As a child, Phoebe's father controlled the family's finances, and boundaries were hazy at best:

> Money was never discussed.... My father handled it and my mother spent it for small consumer goods. He berated her, along with "us girls," for her spendthrift ways, yet he was the one who bought expensive cars, "big boy toys" (every camera and projector ever created, ham radio system)....
>
> I always tried to have my parents use some rules, or some discipline in handling money with me. I remember finally in college I disobeyed them by getting a part-time job ... they actively and repeatedly discouraged me from working. My job was to get good grades.... I almost envied my friends who had some boundaries about their use of money.

After many years of struggling with the contradictions inherent in her upbringing, Phoebe has achieved a measure of clarity concerning the values and attitudes which continue to plague her:

> I was resentful about money, although not conscious about the issues involved. As I have become conscious, as I [have] created a separate identity from my parents—which caused much anguish in my family—I realize how money was used to control us.
>
> My parents have always been churchy do-gooders. They devote their lives to "helping" others. For many years I mistook this for genuine goodness, but as I was able to examine the causes for my deep resentment of my parents, I started to see that all of their generosity toward others served primarily to prove their own worth to themselves.... Their lavish attentions create dependency and

resentment in people. In our many discussions and arguments through the years, my parents have expressed a condescending attitude toward people who "need their help." My mother has an awful habit of calling people she considers needy "little," regardless of their age or size or height.

Phoebe's coming to consciousness has not been without its own repetition of the very attitudes that proved so painful in her early years. Her first marriage was rife with them:

> Money was the source of disagreements. My husband, like my father, would not discuss our finances with me, despite my repeated request to work out a budget together. He, like my father, discouraged me from working full time while the children were young [the son they had together, and his daughter from a previous marriage] and I was writing my dissertation. This was wonderful for me at the moment, but he [also] discouraged me from working full time after my dissertation was complete.
>
> Then, when I decided to divorce him, he started to accuse me of taking advantage of him. He claimed he put me through graduate school, when actually by the time I met him I was only taking one credit of dissertation writing per semester. And, believe it or not, last week—ten years after our separation, and after he remarried twice—he reopened the old issues surrounding money!
>
> In my recent marriage, we have had some discussions about money. My husband is very clear that he assumes I will pay for my expenses, and he will pay for his. He doesn't want to support me at all (even if he could afford to do so, which he cannot as a mental health worker for the State). This is a good policy for preventing the kind of control that my parents and first husband exercised over me through their "generosity."

Still, Phoebe admits, "part of me wants to be taken care of, since I am so used to that." And she is determined to try to give her child a healthier money sense than that which his father and grandparents provide:

> [My son] has chores to do and must pay for some of his hobbies with his own money. He bristles at this idea, since his father and grandparents are all sugar daddies. But he is not a spoiled kid. I think that part of the reason why he does not take his things for

granted is my choice of where to live ... a working-class part of town. His good buddies—all ten or more—are from working families.

[But] it is hard to raise my child to hold my attitudes when his father and grandparents treat him like a potentate. It was also hard to discipline him the way I believed was right when I was married to his father and when my mother stayed with us for two months. But, with the help of my therapist, I have held my own, asserted myself as his mother, and have my standards accepted at my house. And, I have accepted that I cannot control the way my parents and ex-husband treat my son at their houses. He will grow up differently than I would have liked in some ways, but not in all.

Andrea is a mother who has taken great care to give her stepdaughter a strong sense of self. A financial advisor, she has logically seen money management as a terrain on which to pursue this goal. Although we are friends and frequently talk, when she responded to my questionnaire I had my first glimpse of her own childhood experience and the personal struggle that surely played its part in her choice of careers. Andrea describes her parents' origins as "white trash, poor and uneducated." But she is in her mid-forties now and they entered their own version of middle-class life when she was a child:

Neither [of my parents] had a college education. They started out as a machinist and dishwasher.... Mom has always been an overdoer, so she made all of our clothes. She canned fruit and vegetables. They hunted for venison. When we had the space, we had chickens and ducks for eggs and meat (even in town). When we didn't live in town, we had cattle and sheep.

Andrea and her two sisters always worked: odd jobs at home or for other families, such as yard work, baby sitting, even ironing. As both parents eventually moved up into better jobs—her father becoming an optical engineer, her mother the supervisor of the computer division at a scientific laboratory—money continued to be an enigma to this daughter. The family lived in a decent house by then, and had a family car, but nothing was saved for college. Notions of scarcity and exaggerated talk about waste persisted.

Early on, Andrea seems to have found ways to at least attempt to

…

satisfy the needs to which her parents would not give in. In high school she would resist buying a school lunch in order to save for something she wanted. But, although they had a golf club membership, she was unable to convince her mother and father that the swimming pool, where she longed to go, was worth an additional outlay.

> We were not required to save but I always did. My parents bought the necessities, including clothing, but I think they should have given us a clothing allowance instead and made it possible for us to choose our own clothes. Our earnings and allowance were for luxuries, but the amounts were pretty small, so there wasn't enough to really get much. When I got a real job, in high school, my mother tried to prevent me from doing it by saying that I couldn't use the car to go (control again—"I need you to help out around home"), so I rode my bike the first few times and after that she let me use the car. It was [always] a battle, with control of me by her and the inconsistent message about money arose from how it was used as an argument for what she wanted from me.
>
> [This dynamic] instilled a lot of fear in me and there were many places I didn't go and things I didn't do, either because there wasn't money there or I was so fearful of future scarcity that I wouldn't spend it.

These fears played themselves out in Andrea's first marriage and in her handling of money with her husband's daughter. They are present, too, in her thoughts as she begins another important relationship, coincident with responding to my questionnaire. Of life with her husband she says that at first

> I kept things partially separate. We co-owned our house, but after the first couple of years I made the house payment completely, paid all the bills, including his credit card, and gave him any extra money he needed from my checking and savings. He had his separate accounts and his salary to spend on his own expenses.

About her new relationship, with a neurosurgeon, Andrea says:

> There is a closer income situation, but he has much more in the way of expenses and debt and has no equity ownership in anything because he's just starting out. Within the next year we will be going

into what to do about a house. I know ahead of time that will be hard for me, because of my need for security.

But the most interesting things Andrea has to say about money handling concern her relationship with her ex-husband's daughter, who she has mothered from an early age:

> The positive attitudes I think I have passed on to my daughter are to be in control of your own destiny/finances, not to depend on others for any of that, and to plan ahead. She still actively and passively hits me up for money, but when she's done with college that will be over with. I sold her her first car at a very low price and at a low interest rate, so that she would have a stake in the car and its care and would know what it's like to have a monthly obligation that she had to anticipate and plan for. I would say that the jury is still out on how much she learned from that. The car is totally trashed now and she doesn't take care of it. It has had major problems because of neglect and I have paid for repairs because I want her to be safe and have reliable transportation.
>
> I think the best thing I did for our relationship during part of junior high and all of high school was for me to get together with her and figure out what she needed for clothing in a typical year. Then I just gave her that money on a monthly basis. That stopped the dynamic of her asking me for money while we were in stores, asking me to buy her stuff, and me having a stake in what she bought. . . .
>
> A point of contention was her lobbying for more money, not on the basis of what she said she needed but what other kids she knew were getting. This was selectively presented, however, since she went to school with much wealthier and much poorer kids. Like my parents, I put the subject to her on a scarcity basis because initially money was scare and I was also more fearful in the context of the relationship. . . . I wanted her to know "the value of money" and to take control of her destiny in that department, so I encouraged her to have jobs. . . . However, that was another effort that was undercut by her father.
>
> Now I think she has a very good feel for what she needs to anticipate and take care of. Discussing money in relation to school and jobs has generally been constructive and has brought us closer. The more she successfully takes care of her own money business, the happier she seems to be.

Each of us comes to a new living situation with all the insecurities, silences, denial, fear, guilt, unfulfilled needs, and negative practices inherited from earlier periods in our lives. If we are women, these most likely were periods in which we held even less power than we do as adults. Even if they had wanted to, our progenitors probably didn't know how to look at the ways in which they perpetuated the damaging attitudes they themselves inherited. Values frequently come disguised: selfishness made to look like discipline, enabling decked out to resemble help, condescension posing as explanation, a lack of respect passing for discretion, control presenting itself as generosity.

And these issues aren't limited to the personal or individual sphere. Depending upon our class and cultural identities, society defines how we manage money in our communities as well. Going against the rules becomes more difficult the further we stray from the assumptions we've been taught. If we challenge the status quo, recognize choices beyond those we've been "given," break new ground in pursuit of equity or justice, or honor our own creativity, we may experience short-term discomfort. But we help to make life easier for the next generation of women. Like the brave women before us, who were much lonelier because there were fewer of them, hundreds of thousands of us have consciously taken this challenge over the past several decades. The continuing development of feminist theory and practice supports strong collective as well as personal change.

Over a relatively short period of time—in this country barely one or two generations—women's legal status, educational and job opportunities, control of our bodies, capacity for self-examination, and broadening of relationship options have helped dispel some of the mystery around financial matters. Still, old habits and expectations persist. Feminist thought draws on the changes we experience as it provides a language with which we may continue to move forward.

Within the women's movement important attempts have been made at adjusting attitudes and practices to conform to life as we experience it. The sliding scale—more if you can/less if you can't—has been a part of the movement since its beginning. Feminists who run schools, clinics, work as psychotherapists, or offer other services have continued to practice and defend the sliding scale. And, when this form too began to seem arbitrary or inadequate, something called cost-sharing appeared on the scene. Felice Yeskel explains it this way:

> Sliding scales are typically based on a middle-class standard . . .
> reinforc[ing] the "we are all middle class" myth. Many times folks
> on the lower end of the class spectrum cannot afford the bottom of
> the sliding scale and folks on the upper end of the spectrum could
> well afford much higher than the top. . . .[1]

Cost-sharing involves controlled discussions which set the process
within the larger framework of the U.S. class system and the dynamics of
classism. Financial pledges are voluntary, confidentiality is stressed, and
feelings are as legitimate as ideas.

This is particularly interesting in light of something funders and
financial advisors point out: that people with smaller incomes consistently make larger charitable donations and other money gifts to the
causes of their choice than do those who earn more. The feminist development of cost-sharing could change that if it becomes a more generalized practice.

Bridges, A Journal for Jewish Feminists and Our Friends, is experi-
menting with a related change in its policy. It had been publishing for
several years when new funding made it possible to pay contributors for
the first time.[2] In order to be able to continue to do so, the editorial
collective initiated a discussion of options. It admitted that "Coming to a
. . . consensus . . . stirred up deep issues among the editors." Some of the
questions asked were these:

> How do we structure a sliding scale payment system that isn't judg-
> mental but asks people to seriously take into account relative priv-
> ilege, so that those who need the most, get the most? How does it
> feel to pay writers and artists when we as editors (except the
> managing editor) don't get paid? How do other small, alternative
> presses pay their contributors? Do we pay more for prose pieces
> than for poems, more for art than for music? Should we set up a
> sliding scale per manuscript until our money runs out, or just
> divide up what we have?

Bridges came up with a proposal that relies on the individual contributor to decide on her payment by receiving a set amount and then having
the option to donate part or all of it back to a writers and artists fund. In

other words, the editors decided to speak about the issues and then trust each contributor to accept less if she could afford to do so, more if she needed the money. They hoped this would "create an opportunity for all of us to think about class, money, and the contexts in which women write and create—and to do something about the inequalities." These attempts at creating equitable systems, within the family as well as the community, are productive and inspiring, but they often disintegrate when threatened by the larger social milieu. Still, women are at the forefront in attempting change.

And new ways of looking at money, new and more humane experiments in its use, have in recent years moved far beyond sliding scales, cost-sharing, or innovative payment plans. Local currency is one idea that has taken root in Santa Fe, New Mexico; Eugene, Oregon; Syracuse, New York; Kansas City, Missouri; and many other parts of the country. In "The Potential of Local Currency," Susan Meeker-Lowry describes this trend.[3]

In many small towns, she says, people are taking control by creating their own bills, honored in a parallel market and exchanged for goods and services which neighbors provide to one another. Susan Meeker-Lowry quotes economist Thomas Greco, Jr.:

> The proper kind of money used in the right circumstances is a liberating tool that can allow the fuller expression of human creativity. . . . Money has not lived up to its potential as a liberator because it has been perverted by the monopolization of its creation and by politically manipulating its distribution—which makes it available to the favored few and scarce for everyone else.[4]

In places where local currency systems are functioning, wealth is encouraged to stay within the community rather than flow out. A relatively simple bank or central office keeps track of the exchange of bills worth so many hours of gardening or music lessons, so many doctor's visits or pizzas. Of course people must get together to decide upon the relative worth of their commodities and services. But twenty-one communities currently use some form of local currency, and report an increase in business as well as in productivity and feelings of well-being.

People learn once again (if they ever knew) to value themselves beyond what they are commonly paid to do; they come to understand that they have hobbies and other skills they can offer to their neighbors. One community stresses that loans of hours are made without charging interest. Self-reliance and pride are but two byproducts of creating regional economies. In essence, these economies have allowed people some respite from the feelings of greed, competition, scarcity, powerlessness, and inequity engendered by our conventional money system.

Paul Glover, who created the Ithaca, New York local currency project in 1991, describes a typical exchange in which $50,000 has been issued to 900 people. Each Ithaca Hour is worth $10.00, because that's the approximate average hourly wage in Tompkins County. The bills come in five denominations, from a two-hour down to a one-eighth hour note. Everyone who wants to participate is encouraged to do so. Glover says "hour labor cannot enrich people who then take our jobs away to exploit cheap labor elsewhere. It must be respent back into the community from which it comes."

Processes such as these can only be safeguarded by the values and consciousness of their members. Women, and others who have been exploited and manipulated by economies of greed, bear victimization in their flesh. They make excellent authors of change. And each community program gives new range to their creativity and to the ethics of caring that for so long have been used against them.

The following chapter is my story, that of a middle-class white woman with Jewish roots, 58 at the writing, artist, socialist, mother of four, grandmother of six, and late-blooming lesbian. In the process of this book I learned that we become who our parents teach us to be, just as they are products of their own parents' particular blend of courage, fear, subterfuge, and dysfunction. A lot of hard work is necessary to turn negative habits around.

Our work must be rooted in an understanding of patriarchy as well as in a knowledge of how capitalism works. As women we need to lay bare the ways in which we are owned by and attempt to own others. And this isn't always or only about intellectual discovery. It means routing the conditions from our flesh in order to avoid reassigning their damage to those we love—what in the language of sexual abuse work is known as breaking the chain.

The Egg Route   7

the entity called the family—that battleground, open
wound, haven and theater of the absurd, which domi-
nates each human childhood.

—Adrienne Rich

Interdependency between women is the way to a freedom which allows the *I* to *be*, not in order to be used,
but in order to be creative. This is a difference between
the passive *be* and the active *being*.

—Audre Lorde

"Oh he was terrible," my mother said, "he drove Nana Jo to distraction."
She was talking about her father, "a terrible spendthrift."

We became aware of my grandfather's peculiarities through his obses-
sions: vast collections of cameras, socks, monkey wrenches, and luxury
tools he purchased at gentlemen's stores like Abercrombie & Fitch.
Dozens, in some cases hundreds, were found when Mother and her
brother cleaned out his office after his death. Many were in their original
wrappings.

Grandpa DeWitt Davidson had been a jewelry salesman who took his
wholesale gems and settings on the road. He was a traveling salesman,
but not of brushes or encyclopedias. There were stories of a dashing
young man working as a ranger at one of the western parks, among other
such exotic jobs. It was said he was a crack shot, but I never saw guns.
And he raised large dogs.

That Grandpa was a womanizer is an acknowledged family fact.
Growing up, I heard my mother and her brother speak of that aspect of
his life with a sort of benevolent admiration, always noting Grandma's
martyrdom. He eventually became a Christian Science practitioner and

the Second Reader (combination minister/healer) at a prominent New York City church. He was the family patriarch, and thought of as saintly.

Both maternal grandparents were spoken of as somewhat daft. And it is in the spirit of this daffiness myth that my mother spoke. "When I was a child," she said, "Nana Jo had to sell eggs door to door. She had an egg route. That's what a spendthrift Dad was."

I heard this frequently as I grew up, this story about my righteously petulant grandmother. If my mother cared to elaborate, or if I put the egg route comment in context with other bits and pieces of information accumulated over the years, the image conjured looked something like this:

> Nana Jo, with her coarse white hair, darkly-circled eyes, and tense mouth, climbs into the back seat of an elegant chauffeured automobile. Perhaps a Stutz. The driver is uniformed. Nana's small hands, an unpainted half-moon at the base of each nail, hold a large basket: carefully so as not to disturb its fragile contents. The eggs are covered with a linen napkin, maybe a small table cloth folded several times over, almost certainly monogrammed. As this liveried transport makes its way through the privileged streets of Roslyn, New York, I imagine Nana descending and knocking on the doors of mansions like her own.

I may have seen the estate once, as a child. Memories are in conflict on this. In any case Mother often talks about the mansion where she grew up and in recent years longs to go back and see it one last time—its stable, boat house, and lawn sweeping down to a substantial stretch of beach rights on Long Island Sound. Last we knew, William Casey's (ex-director of the United States Central Intelligence Agency [CIA]) family lived there. His widow responded to a note from Mother with a gracious one of her own, in which she assured her she was welcome whenever she might wish to visit.

But back to Nana's egg route. In my imagination and throughout my growing up, I saw her descending and reentering that limousine, descending and reentering, always with the egg basket on her arm. It took me years to question the egg route story, and then I did so with irritation, even anger:

"Mother," I demanded, "why do you keep repeating that crazy story? Doesn't it seem contradictory to you that a woman with a 23-room house would sell eggs door to door? Haven't you ever stopped to ask yourself about the car, the gas, the chauffeur's salary? Any of those expenses would have been more than Nana could have made hawking eggs!"

My mother didn't look at me. "No," she admitted, "not until just now."

*   *   *

My father was the youngest of three sons in a Jewish family of German descent. His mother was first generation, having been born in New York City where he and his two older brothers were also born and grew up. His father came from Munich as a teenager, "with $16 in his pocket." A "self-made man" (repeated definitions are important here), he eventually became co-owner of a company that reproduced quality lithographs for greeting cards, calendars, and candy-box covers.

My father was the baby. Having had two boys, his parents hoped for a girl. It was often mentioned, but never more than in passing, that they made him wear a dress and a large bow on his long blond curls. This was his curse until he was six and started school. I have seen the photographs. But when I asked my father how that made him feel, his response was always: "Oh, it was the times, you know . . . they meant well." I also know that a German governess cared for my father and his brothers, that their mother rarely entered the nursery, and that everyone was surprised when, upon Dad's admission to first grade, it was discovered he could not speak English.

Dad said his father was Prussian and stern of character. He didn't easily communicate with his children, preferring to reward a son or settle a dispute by leaving a ten-dollar bill beneath the boy's pillow at night. Albert Reinthal Sr. died young, before I was born: a heart attack. Perhaps, it was said, provoked by the market crash of 1929.

My paternal grandmother, whom I *did* get to know throughout my early childhood years, remained in lifelong mourning for her husband. I remember an armchair in her somber living room, off-limits because of the broad satin ribbon that came together in a large bow across its seat. This had been Grandpa Albert's chair, and no one was to sit in it, ever. Such objects populate my memories of Daisy Heavenrich Reinthal's Park Avenue apartment. The dark furniture, the musty tapestries and oriental rugs. Some of it later ended up in my parents' home, backdrop to my own childhood.

Nana Daisy had shelves of unopened books, many with heavy leather bindings and gold-leaf lettering: early Book-of-the-Month Club selections. These books were ornamentation, rarely sources of knowledge or pleasure. Family lore said she preferred The Reader's Digest; I remember seeing a copy or two on her polished maple night stand. There was the menacing oil painting of a great- or great-great-grandmother, leaning heavily forward in its ornate frame. She stared us down as we endured Sunday dinners around Nana's table. And there was the finger bowl formed of alternating petals of black and clear glass; once I raised it to my lips, an eager child unschooled in its use.

This grandmother had seductive clothes closets with satin-quilted hangers and little flower-shaped sachets hanging among her dark dresses. Her bureau drawers exuded a scent I easily conjure half a century later: lavender and folded satin, bath salts and wealth. Pale green, dusty rose, and gold were her decorator colors, but the dresses were always dark brown, navy blue, or black. An oval brooch—tiny diamonds set in platinum—adorned her breast or sat at the base of her formidable neck.

I remember a low stool with a cross-stitched cushion beside Nana Daisy's bed. As she languished against lacy pillows, her Irish maid, Agnes, sat on that stool to take dictation of the day's marketing list. Another family story—this one told with my parents' disapproval—had her complaining about Agnes who had been years in her employ: she had forgotten her place and sat on the edge of the bed. Agnes herself fared badly in my grandmother's will. I remember my father telling me that after long years of devoted service she'd been left very little. He led his brothers in a campaign to remedy the situation.

I know nothing of Daisy Heavenrich's childhood or youth, but cannot imagine her as anything but pampered, within the strictures of patriarchal control. Old albums, family stories, and my own childhood memories all evoke a woman who never worked, inside or out of her home. She was taken care of "as a woman should be" and enjoyed using her money to take care of others. I can still see her waving a $10 bill at the head waiter who would show us to a "good" table at Schrafts. This was the late forties, when ten dollars bought an average family groceries for a week. Or the totally inappropriate fur coat she gave me as I awkwardly approached adolescence.

Dad's childhood was always easier for me to picture than Mother's: wealth made ostentatious to compensate for the uneasy stigma of being Jewish. There would be ocean liners and governesses but the right country club was beyond social possibility. In those years Jews might do well at business and wield a certain behind-the-scenes political influence, but they couldn't enter Harvard or be elected to public office. My father, who wanted only to participate in varsity sports and play the cello, was sent to the University of Pennsylvania's Wharton School of Business. His ineptitude and utter lack of interest must have been a disappointment to my grandfather.

I remember one of Dad's early business ventures: a tiny pipe and tobacco shop in downtown New York City. On Saturdays I would ride the commuter train with him and share a can of Campbell's Vegetable Soup and saltines in its cluttered back room. I loved curling my tongue around the little white letters. In our basement in the suburbs I helped Dad blend the tobacco. Its moist aromas are with me as I write.

A great roll of green and white Christmas paper was in the family for years. I suppose Dad bought it in bulk when he opened the business, and what seemed like miles of the stuff remained when it went under. Everyone judged that paper ugly, but my parents wouldn't throw it out; holiday after holiday it was hauled forth and used because it had been paid for. Such was the nature of thrift in the home where I grew up—balls of saved string, little bundles of used rubber bands, the wrapping paper from others' gifts, all carefully removed, folded, and saved.

Dad's oldest brother, Edward, is unevenly present in my memory. As firstborn, he was the executor of the family trust. After his early death the job went to his son Jimmy, not to my father or Uncle Albert. Dad's middle brother was different. Kindly is the word that comes most quickly to my mind. A kind man, easygoing and jovial. But when the others said different they meant something else. I learned he had been struck with encephalitis while in college. Sleeping sickness, it was called back then. He'd been asleep for a year, they said, and always spoke of him as if he "wasn't quite right."

When I had my first child—as a single mother in the New York City of the late fifties and early sixties—the only relatives who embraced us were my Uncle Albert and his wife Jean. They had moved away from Park Avenue's dark corridors and mahogany-lined rooms to a sunny little place on Madison. It was never too much trouble for them to come downtown, way down to the Lower East Side slum where I lived with my son. They would hike up the three dingy flights and visit us there, sometimes even baby-sit when I went out.

Years later Albert and Jean left the city altogether, taking their horses to Maryland where they lived their last years in a senior citizens community of some kind. Albert died in November of 1983. It feels right that the money he left my father should have gone to build the house I live in. Jean must have died sometime later. The way my parents kept track of relatives and old friends was if they received a holiday card. A few years back the cards from Jean stopped coming.

In 1947, when our parents picked up and moved us from East to West, it's as if an invisible line was drawn. They erased the family connections in a single sweep. Or were they the ones erased? Not just distance, but silence. We begin at the threshold of our own lives. Who stopped writing to whom? Who stopped calling? Who wanted to forget? And what was it they wanted to forget?

*   *   *

If money talked in my father's family, it was righteously mute in Mother's. Much harder to figure. Lies perched on the shoulders of lies, until deciphering it all required more investigative ability than a young girl like myself could possibly have. One of the central lies turns out to be ethnic, a product of undeclared anti-Semitism, a self-hatred undoubtedly inherited from her own parents and they from . . . well, who knows. The fact is, I was raised believing that my father's Jewish family did not take to my mother, a gentile, because she was not "one of them." Not one of them because she was not a Jew? Not one of them because her family's money was less stable, or altogether less? The implication was that the former took precedence over the latter, although both were somehow true.

Yet my mother's family *was* Jewish. It included the Davidsons, the Lehmans, the Rosenwalds, and very prominently the Sangers—those

German Jewish brothers who built an empire of department stores on the Texas frontier. Growing up, I never gave much thought to my maternal grandparents' surname, Davidson: Son of David. My mother always said it was Scotch, implying there were no Jews in Scotland. She often spoke about a tartan plaid, symbol of that side of the family. Lehman was my maternal grandmother's maiden name; she was Josephine Lehman. It is fairly recently that I even heard that name.

I was already in school before I would notice and begin to ask questions about our own last name, Randall—different from my paternal grandmother's which was Reinthal. I first became aware of the contradiction when I was six or seven, rummaging through a box of my parents' saved mementos.

> Mother irons one of Dad's white shirts, at the pull-down board in our pantry. I can still see the miniature replica for sleeves and collars, set above its larger version. "I can't find your name," I pout, studying the passenger list of the old S.S. Stavangerfjord. I know my parents took that ship on their honeymoon, and that they traveled third class. I know I am looking in the right place. I go back to the beginning of the list, pronouncing each name again in my child's determined syllables.
>
> Mother stops ironing. My question forces her to explain that their name *is* there, but it is not the one I've been looking for. "It was Reinthal back then," she says, "like your grandmother's." My litany of questions pushes her to say more; Mother subscribes to the school that tells you to give a child only as much information as she shows she is able to understand. But that night I don't think she gets beyond the name-change itself.
>
> Perhaps I ask why. I am always asking why. Perhaps it is then that the myth is born, about it being easier to spell or say. Our exchange dims at this point, but this is the first of years of such conversations: I repeatedly trying to get one or both of my parents to tell me the truth that I intuit; they, out of love and a misplaced protective impulse, uneasiness, shame or all of these, clinging to the fiction they've created.

If only my parents had been able to give me the stories, in all their ugliness, desperation, and fear. And the pride? What happened to the pride? Perhaps it was the missing link. Because they could not articulate what they ran from, why they felt ashamed, how they saw their name-change as panacea in their children's lives, my sister, brother, and I grew up breathing the confusion of ethnic meltdown. The perpetuation of self-hate.

In our several ways and at different times in our lives, my brother, sister, and I have each tried to retrieve the cumbersome history: a knowledge, an image, a recognition, a taste, smell, way of being in the world—retrieve it, or pass it on without ever having had it ourselves. I remember telling my firstborn that we were Jewish; not religious or observant, but that this was a history that also belonged to him. Then, several months after our father's death, Mother finally volunteered the story I'd sought those many years.

> We are going somewhere in my car, a scenario that often provokes a confessional atmosphere. "If you *really* want to know why I changed our family name," she begins—no prologue apparent — I'll tell you."
>
> I wait, silently digesting her use of the personal pronoun.
>
> "It was because of what I suffered as a child, the other kids running after me on my way home from school, shouting 'dirty jew, dirty jew.' I didn't want my children to have to suffer that. It's what made me hate school . . . all my life . . . "
>
> Her sudden admission confirms a fact I had only recently begun to understand, that she made the important family decisions; Dad went along. It also opens a window on my mother's pain, mostly tapped way down so that only the flotsam surfaces. I understand that she was trying to avoid the hurt that comes with jibes, the discrimination from which she thought she was saving us. I want to tell her I appreciate whatever part of her decision came from love, but that I wished she had stood proud, preparing a ground on which we too might stand.

I don't know how to tell my mother any of this. When I commiserate with her about her childhood victimization and try to talk about the terrible power of anti-Semitism, all she can do is agree. The lesson isn't something she can own. But I know this is important to my story, because in some as yet undecipherable way both parents gave their children an uneasiness about our Jewish heritage. And this was linked—again in ways I don't completely understand—to our family's money myths.

What I now know as self-hate and fear masked themselves in my mother's family as a mixture of breeding and culture: definitions consistently misused but clearly forming the core of how my maternal grandmother, especially, wished to be perceived. To her, good breeding and genteel culture meant a well-modulated speaking voice, understatement, conformity, Republican politics, non-Jewishness. Unacceptable, in friends as well as relations, was the person who "slaughtered the King's English"—I imagined a villain with a long knife actually slitting the throat of a biblical calf called English; a king with a crown had the calf on a short rope and tried unsuccessfully to pull it from harm's way. In the presence of these grandparents you didn't speak too loud, dress exuberantly, draw attention to yourself, express original ideas, or feel easy as a Jew (or as a black or a Hispanic or an Indian or an Asian, for that matter—they were racists across the board). Difference might make titillating conversation; there was much travel talk, a fascination with other peoples and places, but always from the colonialist stance.

In the late fifties I moved back to New York as a young woman and incipient writer. My maternal grandmother declared my black stockings and thick eye-shadow a plot to shock and perhaps even do her in. My grandfather, who enjoyed an unearned reputation for benevolence, refused to lend me the $25.00 I needed to purchase a used Remington Rand (at the time and for many years a popular brand of manual typewriter).

When, a few years later and unmarried, I gave birth to my son, some indelible line had been crossed. Nana Jo and Grandpa called my parents to suggest I be "put away." But their curiosity got the better of them and they sent their son, my Uncle DeWitt, downtown to take a look at the child. He came bearing a small plastic duck, a toy Gregory rejected at first sight. He would scream whenever it landed in his bath water. In fact, my usually even-tempered son cried for the duration of his great uncle's visit. Children are wise. It would be a long long time before I would remember what my maternal grandparents did to me as a child. But I no longer needed to pretend we were friends.

In my memory, only one half of the doorframe is illuminated, the other half and the room itself—from where the child, me, sees—is in darkness. Nana Jo leans against that brightened side of the frame, her face, her dark eyes fixed on what is happening inside the room. Happening, no. Being done. Being done to the child, to me.

He pins me against the green lucite top of a clothes hamper, its surface covered with something clean and warm. But my body is held against my will. Frozen. Hurt. Now I am floating somewhere above that small terrified body, experiencing and watching. Refusing to experience. But watching.

The powdery white face descends, that other white head rises: heads, faces, tensed lines of a mouth spilling liquid that will drip onto me, into me, stain me, fill me, undo me, destroy . . . NO!

At the last possible moment I make the necessary gesture, kick or silent scream, brandishing of tiny fists. I succeed in reinventing what I now know to have been his mouth, his penis, his invasion of my self. In that moment my terror of mushrooms is born. The birth of terror.

As my grandmother watches.

She takes it all in—my struggle, his pleasured will, my humiliation and escape. She cannot forgive any of them. But she also takes a witnessed satisfaction. Perhaps this is when she begins to hate me, as she leans against that doorframe, her breathing a staccato harmony.

Incest was another family secret, easier to hide than the Jewish jewelry salesman become Christian Science practitioner, the truth behind the egg route story, my grandfather's bad investment of a great deal of money that her Uncle Isaac Sanger had left to my mother, or how much ordinary things cost. Because now they also had my complicity, purchased in flesh.

My maternal grandparents would be many years dead before I would remember, in therapy, that both conspired to rape me when I was an infant. The unfolding seems a process of forever. Those whose interests are served still protect the perpetrators. But memory about money is like memory about sexual abuse: both lead down a road of reclaimed power.

Now a web of financial lies crumbles like the cover-up of incest once did: a further peeling away of mockery and myth.

Where I remember visiting these grandparents, they had clearly come to less. They lived in a modest apartment in New York's Tudor City, a grimly proper midtown neighborhood in the area of the United Nations. There were separate parks for adults, children, and dogs. Grandpa's office was a short walk away, across from the 42nd Street Library. There, in a small suite of rooms, he dispensed his Christian Science healing mostly to wealthy older women, had a few precious stones and gold settings still locked away in the safe, and stored those fearsome collections.

Gone was the many-roomed mansion with its series of out buildings; "any one of which you would have been proud to call home," my mother always said. Gone the Stutz and its uniformed chauffeur. Gone too my mother's inheritance, except for a monthly $100 check with which her father presumed to pay back his debt to her. At their parents' death only my uncle inherited. It didn't really matter, everyone including Mother said, as she had a husband who would care for her.

I've wondered about the effect my grandparents' change of fortunes might have had on Mother's life. The various stages remain somewhat unclear. The facts seem these: Grandpa "lost everything" at one point, and was forced to move his family from the Roslyn mansion. "Was your standard of living dramatically altered?" I've asked, trying to account for Mom's admitted desire to "marry well."

But she says it wasn't that. "We moved to the Belnord in the city," she remembers, and goes on to describe its elegance. How did my grandfather climb back up again? That is, if the total-loss story is to be believed. Later research suggests he may have borrowed large sums of money from other family members, and that he rarely paid them back. Then there were the fees he must have received from wealthy widows in his practice as a Christian Science practitioner. Perhaps no single jolt accounts for Mother's fears and inhibitions. Surely having been born into that family would have been enough.

Perhaps my mother survived her upbringing in part by retreating into herself. I have come late to a recognition of her shyness; it was too often hidden behind a facade of banter and charm. Her obsessive parents must have permanently thwarted her intellectual curiosity. She is perfectionist in her endeavors, but unquestioning of even the most obvious mind traps, a chronic but unexamined frustration hovering beneath congenial conversation. My mother is a small, slim woman who wears no make-up and rarely gets a professional haircut. She is very handsome, enjoys being admired, and frequently is.

Mother, like Dad, could also be lavishly generous—generous in important ways that have meant a better life for her children. She is generous because she genuinely enjoys giving and also because—as was true of her parents before her and continues to be a problem for those in my generation—the gifting has become a language of approval or of care. When the money says "I love you best" or "I approve of what you just did" or "I want you to do something for me," that's when it all goes wrong.

As I grew I would learn something—never enough—about my mother's artistic endeavors. I know she quit a school for young ladies, which she detested, by simply announcing to her parents that she would not go back. It was then that she entered New York's Art Students League, where she studied with several well-known teachers. Although as a child she hated school (the kids who chased her, shouting "dirty jew"), she says those years studying art were among the best of her life.

She became a monitor, helping the other students prepare their clay and build their armatures. The professors personally conducted their classes only once a week. Mom says she loved the teaching and an infrequent light charges her tired eyes. She wanted to be a sculptor. A few examples of her work from that period graced my childhood home: two or three classical busts cast in bronze and a more "utilitarian" pretzel holder in the shape of a long-necked giraffe, also bronze.

Mother's memory hesitates now, around some of the precise dates and other details of that long-ago time. But probably coincident with her attendance at the Art Students League she and a friend named Lucille worked at Palmenberg's on Broome Street. She says they were fifteen and lied about their age to get into the League as well as secure the job. At Palmenberg's they built the armatures and modeled the clay figures which, when cast, would be among the country's first department store mannequins.

Throughout Mother's life, this was her only paid employment. She says she earned $125.00 a week, a great deal at the time. But the job was short-lived. When summer came, her family vacationed in Rangely, Maine. It never occurred to her not to accompany them that year, and so she quit. "When I returned, someone else was making the $125.00," she sighs.

Coming from the family she did, one has to admire my mother's curiosity, her ability to make and do. From young adulthood well into middle age she took some interesting risks. It was Mother's idea to leave the suburbs of New York, where Wednesday night dinners had become a tired symbol of all the ways in which she and my father felt stifled by their families. The five of us traveled the country in an old black Studebaker that summer, searching for a place to live. Our parents were seduced by the Southwest.

In New Mexico, Mother threw herself into an exploration of land and culture. Memories of taking old clothing to Indian reservations and trading it for turquoise and silver shame me now, but for my parents, fresh from the East, this was high adventure and a love of beauty. Less painful are my recollections of Mother digging her own clay in Jémez or along the banks of the Río Grande, then bringing it home to refine and use. I loved watching her sift and wash the earth, taking its properties and making art.

Called upon to describe my mother of those years, I would have said bright, spunky, fun-loving, a good mother. As Dad was a good father. Back East, when I was seven or eight, I had begged my Mother for a Girl Scout knife, a thick-bladed combo with bottle-opener and a number of other features in a garish green mother-of-pearl case. I think it cost a dollar at the local Five and Dime. She wouldn't give in. Perhaps she planned on giving it to me for Christmas or my birthday. Or maybe she just didn't want me having a knife.

But I wasn't taking no on this one. I stole the coveted object, then told my mother I had been given it by my Scout leader for meritorious participation. Mom was so proud. When she ran into my school principal she was quick to exclaim upon her daughter's achievement. That's how I was discovered and got dragged before the store manager, knife in hand, its pearly brilliance considerably dulled.

My father and mother succeeded in nurturing a family much more open and feeling than either of their own. Through our childhoods, they moved us light years from the early strictures they'd endured. My father took care of us all, first by working at one unsuccessful business venture after another, later as a public school music teacher, and always and most ably with the interest from those investments made possible by his family inheritance.

Dad financed our life in the New York City suburbs of White Plains, Hartsdale, and then Scarsdale. He paid for the move to New Mexico in 1947: I was ten, my sister seven, and my brother almost three. His family money underwrote our summer trips, which were mostly Mother's ideas: to Europe, to South America on a freighter, to Alaska via the Inland Passage and then driving back along the Alcan Highway. Those adventures are a memorable part of my childhood.

My father had the money, inherited or earned. He managed it. He alone knew how much of it they possessed. My mother had very little of her own, because she never worked outside the home, because her father stole what inheritance she'd been given as a child, and because she herself agreed to getting nothing from her parents' will; after all, she had a husband who looked after her needs.

Mother would often say she wanted a particular item and then not buy it, taking what seemed like a strange pleasure in that denial. At other times she bought things without mentioning them to my father. I believe he would have given her anything. To this day she tends to talk poor, seems unable to understand that she can afford almost anything she wants and certainly whatever she needs.

My brother, sister, and I grew up believing Dad knew everything there was to know about financial matters. And we asked his advice—about credit, savings, investment, insurance. He had gone to the Wharton School, after all, and he once did some menial job on Wall Street—swept ticker tape, or worked as a gofer for a large financial institution. Over the years family lore exaggerated this to his having "worked in New York's financial district," but even such scant knowledge as may have existed was not passed on.

As daughters, my sister Ann and I "didn't need to know." Neither was our brother Johnny given much information, although, as the son, he was eventually named executor of their estate. My brother grew up with a marked aversion to and ineptitude about business, unfortunate since he chose to operate an independent bookstore. Over fifty now, he still struggles to acquire the skills and also to understand how our mother's distaste for people in business—the "Jewish shopkeeper," the working class in general—have informed his own prejudices and affected his abilities.

Dad's deeply rooted fear of authority was something else we all noticed and had to struggle against in ourselves. He was intimidated by the government in its various agencies, the cop on the beat, even by the professionals he paid to do his taxes or provide his insurance. Before he died, in the sad confines of a nursing home, he feared the orderly who put him to bed each night. I saw my father repeatedly humiliated by this fear and raged at its hold on him.

Mother tells us she was in the dark about the money she and my father had—some strange combination of her husband's management style and her own disinterest or disdain. In my family of origin the man earned the living; the woman did not have a job outside the home. My father and mother subscribed equally to this traditional setup. Appearances were important. But just beneath the surface, the classic model took some rather unusual turns.

For example, I don't remember Dad ever assuming a macho stance around the house. He was essentially a gentle man, perhaps too gentle and accepting for his wife's tastes. After a long day selling men's clothing, and later as a public school music teacher, he did his share of house-work, notably more than other fathers I knew.

In spite of the fact that my father was the person who during my child-hood really made me believe in myself, was the one who told me I could do anything I wanted and showed tremendous pride when I did, under-neath the encouragement he thought women were to be cared for. Throughout his life he retained a traditional concept of men's responsi-bility for supporting the women in their lives.

Maybe he lived on the cusp, having inherited the old ideas but embracing the new where and how he could. The old ideas surfaced when he bought life insurance policies for each grandchild as he or she came along. The boys' policies were worth twice what the girls' were worth, "because the girls will get married, you know; they'll be taken care of." Dad's ability to change was reflected in his respect for and encouragement of the different paths his children chose.

No doubt affected by her own childhood socialization, my mother imbued our household with a craziness about money; I can only describe it that way. Sales were important: Mom would pour over the daily paper and note them with care, clipping coupons and making lists of where to go to get each item at the greatest savings. No thought was given to the time it took to visit these disparate stores, nor the gas consumed in doing so. She had no sense that the sales themselves were ruses of a fabricated system.

When I was in junior high, I remember Mother purchasing 100-pound drums of powdered milk. Her repeated explanation of how much we saved with every glass we drank embarrassed us in front of our friends. She prided herself on buying bloody eggs and horse meat rather than beef. "No one can tell me you can tell the difference," she would insist.

Our household would have been judged thrifty by the standards of most of our class contemporaries. We children often wore hand-me-down clothes. My sister's at least came from another child: me. Mine came from some aunt or adult friend of my mother's; they were gathered and pinned and bulkily hemmed and still never seemed remotely in style.

My parents bought second-hand cars. We acquired our first radio, phonograph, and electric blender much later than neighbors or friends. My sister and brother had been watching television across the street for several years before our parents finally relented—after I moved away from home—and bought the family's first 11-inch black and white TV. Still, summer would appear and we'd embark on trips the likes of which our friends' families could not have dreamed.

Even as we made those extraordinary summer journeys, an elaborate explanation about where the money came from was hauled out as justification. We'd hear it repeated even to those who didn't ask. The story was that we saved all winter and then took advantage of my father's long vacations from teaching. In retrospect it is hard to see how anyone could have believed that the pennies saved by drinking powdered milk or eating bloody eggs produced the thousands of dollars needed for each of those trips. Especially on a music teacher's salary. But of course it was important that no one know about my father's inheritance or think us rich. So the myth was born, we repeated it, and for much too long believed it ourselves.

My parents' attitude about money was always different from those of my schoolmates' parents. I quickly graduated from the weekly allowance of the times to a larger clothes allowance. I think I was about twelve when I assumed this responsibility. In retrospect it seems one of the more intelligent programs my parents came up with—teaching me a kind of money management I still find useful. My sister, three years younger, remembers the same system, though less rigorously enforced.

The idea was that I would learn how to apportion what I was given, and it had to cover everything. I remember budgeting carefully, saving from each month's stipend so as to have enough for a pair of shoes or the inevitable yearly winter coat. But I don't remember a correspondingly difficult experience if I failed to save enough for what I needed. Perhaps I never failed to do so.

In spite of my adolescent clothes allowance, in memory what covered my body continued to seem awkward and ill fitting; nothing ever felt quite right. My physical development lagged embarrassingly behind that of my girlfriends, rapidly changing fads stuck in my childlike craw, and in spite of my parents' resistance to commercialism I was being socialized to long for the inbred and unobtainable quality clothing of the rich. There was that deep red formal, reduced on sale my senior year of high school. All the other girls wore pastel pink, powder blue, or white. I can still evoke the body gesture with which I sucked in my belly and thrust my incipient breasts to where I prayed they would hold its velvet bodice up.

Pondering the role that gender may have played in my parents' scheme to teach me how to organize and save, I recently asked my brother if he, too, had been given a clothes allowance in his teens. He couldn't recall. "Maybe. . . . " He stopped. "I remember you having one, but I don't know about me. It wouldn't have made much difference, though. If I'd had trouble making do, Mom and Dad would probably have given me more."

Johnny went on to do some reminiscing of his own: "You know," he said, "I can't remember ever buying clothes for myself. Not really. In thirty years I don't think I've gone into a store for more than a couple of sets of underwear." He explained that as he and my father came to wear the same size, even in shoes, Dad just passed on what he didn't need. Sometimes our father would find shoes he liked and buy two pair. To this day my brother rarely purchases clothes.

Early understanding I would be a writer, I wanted a typewriter of my own. Long before my grandfather refused to lend me the money to buy that second-hand Remington in New York, I had my eye on my first machine: a Royal portable whose smell of inked cotton, 3-in-1 Oil, and darkly textured metal still lives in my fragmented memory of those years. I must have been nine. "Earn half of what you need," my parents said, "and we'll make up the rest." It wasn't about what they could afford. It was, again, about teaching me the value of money. I babysat their friends' children. I remember a starting salary of 25 cents an hour. I sold boxed candy door to door. I had a short-lived paper route. My half of that typewriter came to $75.

Neither the clothes allowance nor the joint typewriter purchase, though, adequately describe how money was treated in our family. I may have been the guinea pig for systems that broke down later when my sister or brother came along, but the deeply remembered sense we all retain is one of frugality: "take care of the pennies and the dollars will take care of themselves."

My brother collected coins. As a small boy he would be ushered into the safe-deposit cubicle at the bank, where he would examine one by one a roll of pennies or quarters; he knew which were worth what, and how to build his collection. "I used to spend all weekend doing that," he tells me now. "It was painstaking work, and I was good for my age. But an interesting thing happened. At a certain point, Dad himself began buying valuable coins. I remember him telling me that when I got my Ph.D. they'd be mine. When I was thrown out of the program just before I was supposed to finish, he gave them to me anyway. He must have felt sorry about what happened."

My sister and I have suffered the pain of sibling jealousy, and my memories of her childhood are less precise. As I write this, though, I am struck by how very differently the three of us handle money today. Although our parents' finances remained steady as each of us grew up, gender, birth order, and character idiosyncracies must be important in defining our several approaches.

I tell my partner Barbara, "I perceive of Ann as having the most, because she's the only one of us who owns her own home. She's worked at the same job for many years, has health care and other benefits. Security. She and her husband have a motor home . . . " and I continue to enumerate pieces of a lifestyle that is stable, though certainly not luxurious.

"No," Barbara disagrees, her own working-class background coming to the fore. "I perceive of *you* as having the most money, even though you don't own any of those things, or have a job or benefits. I think of you as having more money because I see you as the more powerful."

Money as power. No getting away from it.

Johnny has spent much of his adult life trying to make a go of an

independent bookstore. Since his divorce, he lives in a one-room effi-
ciency apartment. It's easy to see him as having less because he does.
But I am interested in Barbara's observations about money and power.
"You know my financial situation," I prod, "How can you equate power
with money in my case?"

"I'm not saying I equate it," she insists, "I'm saying that's the way it's
perceived. Yes, even by me. Look at what you spend your money on:
travel, art, the things most people buy *after* the basics have been covered.
You take off for South America or Europe, have a daughter at Smith
College. . . . No matter that most of your travel is work related, and Ana's
got what amounts to a full scholarship. These are things that give a
perception of wealth. And power."

I know she's right. And I wonder, again, how each of us got where we
are. I think of the policy I've evolved over more than thirty years, of
spending a quarter of what I make from the sale of my art on the work of
younger women artists. As faithful as a tithe. Who or what started me on
that? Perhaps the commitment took root during my time among the
Abstract Expressionists in New York, where I had my first lessons in
mentoring. It may also have been nurtured by my parents' attitude of
encouragement, especially my father's.

And I think of *how* we spend our money. I mean the mechanisms we
use. My brother and I have never bought anything on time. Even with
large purchases, we save until we can buy outright: certainly our parents'
influence. My sister acquires big items in installments: a characteristic of
the lower-middle or working class, Barbara says. Johnny points out that
the very rich also borrow to spend—important to their power of acquisition. And I think: in the United States today almost everyone has been
forced into a system of credit by consumerist propaganda, engineered
obsolescence, debt as a way of life. Our parents never bought in installments. Either you had the money or you didn't. I can still hear Dad's
words of advice, unmindful of the fact that most people would be unable
to follow them.

My parents consistently talked poor, backed up by the bloody eggs, the
powdered milk, the hand-me-downs. Yet they were extraordinarily generous with their children. Sometimes Dad would surprise us with an offering of money. Often, though, it was Mother to whom we found it easier
to go with our need. She then promised she would convince our father, or

"talk him into" the gift. It may have been her genuine concern. It may also have been a pattern she nurtured as a way of buying indispensability. We all encouraged it, of course.

In recent years, since Barbara and I have taken over their finances we've discovered that Mother really never did know much about them. Did he refuse to include her? Did she resist learning? Was this his area of control, when he clearly controlled so little else?

And Dad, although beautifully generous as I've said, often linked some interest of his own to the gifts he bestowed. He might write one of us a check and, as he handed it to us, say: "You can spend this any way you want, of course, but ... " The but may have pointed to something we'd have done anyway, or to something we would never have thought of doing.

Something I'll always carry with me, like a nervous tic, is our parents' expectation, each time we emerged from a restaurant, that each of us personally thank Dad for the meal. This continued way beyond our childhoods, until he went into the nursing home. It wasn't simply an expectation, it was an unspoken demand, and one that seemed strangely out of character in a man who asked almost nothing for himself. It became a family ritual: each of us uttering the words and he shrugging them off with a smile.

> We get up from the table: "Uh, Daddy, thanks for the dinner," one of us says.
>
> "Don't mention it." He smiles.
>
> We are walking towards the restaurant door. Another of us speaks: "Hey, Dad, that was really good. Thanks."
>
> He half turns, looks back. "You're entirely welcome. I'm glad you liked it."
>
> We are crossing the parking lot now, almost to the car: "Well, thanks, Daddy." It's the last voice to be heard.
>
> "Oh ... sure. Don't mention it. Don't mention it."
>
> I breathe a deep sigh of relief. I and everyone else have spoken. Home free.

It had to *seem* casual. But if we failed to do this, the fault was quickly brought to our attention—the underlying assumption being that Dad worked hard to support his family. Mother's contribution, like so many women's, was invisible. The meal had been a gift from the breadwinner. And it was to him that our gratitude must be expressed.

As I grew older, I realized that this matter of acknowledging a gift was central to our lives in a way it was not in other families I knew. Elaborate thank-you notes were an essential response to birthday or Christmas gifts, or to any attention received. These were expected to exceed a line or two of mere acknowledgement—that would have been considered tacky—and to avoid at all costs the ready-made Hallmark message which was thought of as unoriginal and cheap. We were taught to keep lists as we opened each present, and to respond at length: easy for me since I already fancied myself a writer. I got high family marks for my rapidity and for my "sincere and interesting" missives.

Indeed, in this warped pattern never far removed from a strategy of control, gifting became reward, and failure to give a kind of punishment. As I've grown into my own values I've become aware of the strange imbalance between my parents' enormous generosity—crucial help in hard times, substantial support during my immigration battle,[1] the gift of a home—and the way they handled insignificant sums.

During their later years, for almost a decade, we lived next door to one another in the foothills outside Albuquerque. We naturally made it a habit of offering to pick up a bottle of milk or some bread when one of us went into town. They would insist on paying, or being paid, the $1.69; I preferred to let it go. No, not simply preferred. Their insistence on this sort of accounting irritated me almost irrationally. I just couldn't under-stand it within a family, or among friends.

We also would occasionally go shopping together, and Mother always made a big deal about who should put the dime or quarter in the parking meter; it depended on whose errand it was. If one of my long-distance calls appeared on their telephone bill, my father especially would bring the item to my attention—even if it was $4 or $5. "I'm not asking you to pay it right now," he'd begin, but it was clear that he wouldn't be able to relax until I did. A couple of days later, he might surprise me with a check for $1,000.

*   *   *

Early on I knew I had to escape the tensions of my parental home. The pressures were subtle, so they were that much more difficult to identify. Indeed, I always thought of my parents as special, much more permissive and understanding than those of my friends. I was barely eighteen when I married for the first time: a bad marriage but the only way I must have imagined I could escape from a difficult situation that was defined as so ideal.

I ran for a very long time.

With that same young husband and $400 I rode a motor scooter down through central Europe to Spain. Later we divorced and I lived four years in New York City. That's where I began to learn about art, discipline, and politics. Late fifties, early sixties: the country still smelled of prosperity, at least for those from the middle and upper-middle classes. Anything was possible. And there was plenty of time.

I was too young to be worried about old age. Money was to subsist on; art became central. Income was what you needed to buy time for the important work; in my case that meant writing. Out of choice, my friends and I lived in lofts and cold-water flats, often on unemployment for as long as the law allowed. We felt we had a right to hustle the State, to one-up the power company or take something we needed from a large department store or corporation. We knew they were stealing from us. We spent what we had on the tools of our artistic trades.

My son resulted from my fervent desire to be a mother and a couple of nights with a fellow poet. Gregory was born in New York and I managed all possible contortions to be able to work and support him. His first six months I talked our way into a daycare program for unwed mothers and their infants at the elegant uptown Dalton School. When he was six months old, we were no longer eligible. Then I persuaded Jewish Philanthropies that he deserved its attention even though he'd been circumcised by a doctor rather than by a rabbi. All the while Nancy Macdonald, my friend and boss at Spanish Refugee Aid, was happy to stretch my hours around any routine that worked for us all.

My three daughters were born in Mexico City, where I went at the end of 1961. There I married again: a Mexican poet who fathered two of them. We translated comic books and put our energies into a bilingual literary journal that flourished throughout the sixties. But I ended up raising all four of my children in Cuba, where I lived from 1969 through the end of 1980. By that time I was divorced again, living with the North American father of my youngest, working as an editor and writer.

Money occupies a very different place in a socialist society. In the Cuba of the seventies, education, health care, and recreation were free. Rent could not legally exceed 10% of a person's salary, and such issues as insurance, investment for the future, or what would happen to us when we got old weren't concerns. The socialist State took care of people.

The revolution's early idealists had dreamed of a society in which money would hardly play a role, a movement from dependant capitalism to absolute community without having to pass through the necessary socialist stage. I remember visionaries like Haydeé Santamaría[2] talking excitedly about the fact that Havana's pay phones had recently been disconnected from their coin boxes and bus fares were down to five cents. These dreams, and many larger ones, were dashed over the years as the Cubans struggled to diversify a one-crop economy and lessen their dependance on others. From the beginning, the U.S. government worked, and continues to work, at destroying what the Cuban revolution's own mistakes didn't. Still, almost four decades later, Cuba remains the only Latin American country where equality and community are palpable goals.

I have only been in Cuba a couple of months. I was ill when I arrived, and now require surgery for a serious kidney problem. Still I am excited, curious, going into my journalist mode with everyone I encounter.

The middle-aged black woman mopping the floor of my hospital room asks how I feel. I tell her better, thank you, and inquire about her life. "If you had to tell me what this revolution means to you," I ask, "what would you say?"

She stops mopping and looks at me. Her face is radiant: "Honey, this revolution let me marry for love," she says, "you tell me that's not something! I was scared to leave my first husband, scared I wouldn't be able to make it with my kids. Now I can work. I'm independent, my kids got food, and I'm married for love. You tell me that's not something big!"

During the sixties and seventies there was no such thing as unemployment in Cuba, and every worker could count on a month's vacation in twelve. My partner of those years and I took our children to the beach, where almost anyone could rent a fully furnished house for a week or two. During that period in my life I learned to relax about my family's well-being in ways impossible for most of my stateside friends.

Of course there was a flip side to this security: a struggling and threatened socialism tended to level individual difference. There wasn't a lot in the stores. We all had access to the same meager clothing and shoes, with children getting the most. Birthdays meant an extra ration of soft drinks and a cake. International Children's Day in June, which had replaced a religiously based Christmas as a time of yearly gift-giving, featured two toys costing less than three dollars and one costing more for every child in the country. It's hard not to wonder what society the Cubans might have achieved had they not been forced to deal with every variety of U.S. hostility along the way.

This humane economic structure, so different from what I had known, gradually led me to different attitudes about money. I undoubtedly retained some sense of the privilege with which I had grown up: anything is possible and, one way or another, everything will turn out all right. But added to this was the knowledge that comes from *feeling* a part of the system that feeds you.

We'd join volunteer workers digging potatoes on a Friday and by the following Monday those potatoes were at our neighborhood grocery store, waiting to be doled out in rations that would find their way to our hungry dinner tables. This direct involvement with cause and effect along the food chain offers a sense of belonging hard to describe or duplicate in a capitalist economy, except perhaps in small experimental communes or collectives. A creative power. Anything is possible, yes, but not just for the privileged few—for everyone.

Living, working, and raising my children under socialism quickly brought me to the point where I believed that I coded and decoded money issues differently from my parents. With my own children, I thought, I had learned to be more open and honest. I would never use money as a tool of control. And I am sure that the Cuban experience did affect me deeply. I have never, for example, looked at a homeless person and wondered why he or she didn't have a job. I see shelter, food, health, education, and a great deal more as rights that everyone should be able to expect.

Now, after long struggles with all my offspring, though, I can see that money-as-metaphor transcends even such profound differences as those which separate socialism from a free market economy. One is shaped by one's political philosophy, but early discomforts and fears persist, surfacing at moments of sudden change or stress.

It can take a lifetime, as my partner often tells me, for someone who was made to feel she cost too much as a child to ever really believe she deserves even that which she herself earns. In my case, it wasn't about fearing I cost too much, but about having learned to control others through the giving or withholding of money. It was an attitude I would long remain blind to, just as my parents were unable to see it in themselves. The difference is that I am fortunate to live at a time when we have found ways to examine such issues, modify lifelong practices, and change habits so damaging to our relationships and to ourselves.

It's still about power.

In New York, Mexico, Cuba, and Nicaragua, I was a sometimes partnered, sometimes single mother, always the center of my children's economic and emotional well-being. In Cuba, the State assumed a great deal of the responsibility. In Nicaragua, where I eventually moved with my two youngest daughters, we struggled along with many others in a mixed economy where some needs were equitably met and others remained unfilled. Throughout, unconsciously or even consciously, I spoke loud that language of punishment and reward. I can remember threatening to withhold an allowance from a child who disobeyed, then retreat from the threat, perhaps offering extra compensation as I struggled to "buy" his or her love.

I remember vowing never to cause my youngest the pain of bad-mouthing her father, against whom I felt a righteous yet unresolved rage. But when I had to work hard to provide her—and the other three—with the basics, and he sent no child support but lavished her with birthday luxuries, I forgot that vow and shrieked the unfairness of it all. A red Baby Doll nightie with white polka dots and eyelet trim remains a vivid image; shoes had been especially difficult that year.

When my children were young it was easier for me to talk about how men abandon their parental responsibilities and move on to younger women than it was for me to see how the money attitudes we all inherit perpetuate messages that are horribly mixed. If I owe my changed perceptions and attitudes to anyone, it is largely to my youngest daughter, Ana. She suffered, as we all have, from the manipulation that passes from generation to generation, within whatever class and culture. Leaving the war in Nicaragua and coming to a consumerist United States at the age of 14 probably helped push things into sharper focus for her. I know it capsulized her experience.

My daughter's story is hers to tell, or not. I must resist my desire to overstep her boundaries. Enough to say that when we were able to talk to one another about some of the damage passed down, when we were able to redevelop and deepen the relationship that had become too painful for us both, she gave me an extraordinary gift: the opportunity of going back and trying to deal with my own issues around money.

"I *need* to be in the book," my daughter Ana says suddenly, "for it to come full circle. I see that now."

We are driving from Montreal down to her home in western Massachusetts, through the burgeoning green of an early Vermont spring. Twenty-six, beautiful, competent, she is at the wheel; I am in the passenger seat beside her. A week or so before our visit I had sent her a draft of this manuscript, eager to know if she would read and comment. She has almost finished it now, and this is the beginning of her response.

Necessary background moves us through years of money inhibition and discomfort to an earlier draft in which I had exposed our conflicts and she had come back quickly with an angry "that's *my* story. I don't want you using it in your book." Later in the process I sent her a copy of my questionnaire; she didn't respond. Now, after reading most of what I've written, she feels ready to talk about what she's felt.

She sees that her point of view is important, necessary to understanding how one generation affects the next. But her willingness to engage is also the result of years of mutual struggle. It has meant hard work on both our parts. At this moment, as the New England landscape whizzes by, we've arrived at a place where honest exchange is possible. The next question is how best to record the exchange.

"Too late for an interview . . . " I think out loud, "maybe I could take some notes." "Ummm . . . " she responds, and keeps on driving. And talking. Fertile farm country unfolds to either side of our moving car, bordering Interstate #91. Miles vanish as we charge ahead, and sentences come fast upon one another, one often barely finished before the next comes tumbling out. I am conscious of resisting the impulse to finish hers, letting her words settle in their own space. "I can't remember the order of things," my daughter starts. Neither can I, but the feelings are very present.

And so we talk—from the Canadian border all the way into Northampton, Massachusetts—about the ways in which I have made her feel unseen and disrespected. About how my money issues have invaded her life. About my providing aid in times of crises only to follow those "gifts" with a constant pointing out of the ways in which I've seen her out of control: spending beyond her means or on things of which I cannot approve. About our struggle around school: the monies offered and "interest" demanded, in inquiries about grades, living expenditures, extras. "Well, how much *do* you have in the bank?" I had once asked.

"I always felt like you disapproved of me," she says. "When I wanted to make a small trip or buy something I didn't absolutely 'need.' Need by *your* standards. Like I was afraid to tell you I was going to Miami on my break that time, remember? Or even that I'd splurged on a massage. . . . But it's because you do the same thing, you know. And not just with me. So often you hesitate when talking about a trip you want to make, or something you want to buy. As if you were ashamed. At your age you should feel okay about spending the money you earn. You've worked hard enough. You have a right to enjoy it without expecting recriminations. And I demand that right for myself."

I remind Ana that at a certain point she had asked me to stop sending her the monthly college stipend. For five or six months no monies passed from my hands to hers. She felt that she needed time to organize her own earning and spending without having to worry about my thinly veiled conditions, my cajoling or condemnation. She didn't want the burden of forced account-ability. I remember making an effort, during those months, to continue our weekly contact without bringing up the issue of money. I refrained from asking her how she was doing, waited for her to broach the subject.

Eventually she did. A semester was coming to a close and a new one rearing its needful head. During one of our cross-country phone conversations, Ana quietly asked if I would be willing to resume sending her the agreed-upon amount each month. Just as quietly, I said I would. Low-key like that. And I remember taking unspoken stock of the fact that I wasn't even *curious* about how she was managing her funds. I liked the feeling. She'd been work-ing right along, as well as making Honors ever since she'd been in school. Clearly she was doing just fine.

But our conversation as we passed those gentle New England hills goes deeper than Ana's college experience. We talk about her childhood. She reminds me of when, upon receipt of a check from their grandparents, I would urge her and her siblings to write those famous thank-you notes. A painful continuation of the notes that I, as a young girl, had been made to write. More often than not the thanks outshone the presence of the gift itself. Now Ana articulates what I have only intuited: "I really think your insistence on those notes helped create a distance between my grandparents and me," she says. "It kept me from ever getting really close to them."

The images come in quick succession now as Ana reminds me of the times I would arrive with an expensive gift—when she was hurting for the rudiments of living. Perhaps my unspoken message was: I can afford this sort of luxury, and you'll just have to learn how to make it on your own. My way of "teaching responsibility"? Or an unexamined perpetuation of the ways in which I myself have been conditioned? Surely that excessive gift-ing screamed "look at me.... look at what I'm giving you ... love me ... please!"

The mother/daughter relationship is certainly one of the most complex there is. We mothers grow old learning to completely let go of that person most like ourselves, that developing being who originated within our bodies and may closely mirror the subtlest nuances of our spirit. The mother fights an ongoing battle against trying to make of the daughter the woman she has lost the chance to grow into. The daughter wants one thing and one thing only: total trust. Nothing less is acceptable.

In our family what Ana calls "the frugalness myth" became the armature supporting a great deal of dysfunctionality. My parents talked poor— to teach us the value of money, to imbue us with a sense of responsibility and accountability, to keep us from believing we could always come to them to get out of a jam. Yet we did come to them when we needed help, and they were always willing to give it.

I continued this myth with my own children; on the one hand making sure they knew I "didn't have enough," while offering gifts that belied the image I attempted to maintain. At the same time, at least in Ana's sense of things, I seemed unable to acknowledge her deepest needs. Finally having struggled our way to a place where we can talk about this issue with only minimal discomfort, my daughter and I find that impediments in other areas of our relationship have melted in the process. An unburdened closeness is sudden evidence of how money remains a metaphor for so much else.

Timing is important here. I mean the age we inhabit. Without years of feminist theory and activism, I wouldn't have been able to put the pieces together. Without my own memory work, in the context of the movement around childhood sexual abuse, I might not have understood the role of memory in recovery. Without an awareness of how racism shapes us all, I would not have been able to look at the anti-Semitism in my family. Without my coming out as a lesbian and finding a partner with whom I can explore these issues on a deeper than intellectual level, I probably would have remained in the succession of unhealthy relationships for which I had been programmed.

And without my father's slow lapse into the swamp of Alzheimer's, I might not so thoroughly have articulated the questions, or some of the answers, that float to the surface of a lifetime of money make-believe. His illness and death precipitated changes in our family structure. In some ways I became my parents' parent. All sorts of myths were exposed. I also like to think that without my generation's struggles, my daughter's generation could not have come so much earlier than we did to a place of agency and hope. Ana's work is her own, but I know she agrees that the chain has been broken and the lessons passed on.

Late in 1983, just before my return to the United States, my father's brother Albert died. The inherited money would build a house for me to live in, he said, on a small piece of land beside his own. Would I like that? The mountain ridge, the cholla and chamisa, the clear light of early morning beside my parents' adobe home: all seemed a welcome respite along a difficult road. I eagerly accepted.

Barbara and I had six or seven comfortable years as my parents' neighbors. When it came to our space, my mother and father were deeply respectful. They always called before coming over. We shared dinners once or twice a week. Dad showed us the trail he walked daily with his aging German Shepherd, and shyly brought us two small barrel cacti he dug up in those foothills. Despite their idiosyncracies and their difficulty in getting along with one another—something that continued to affect my brother, sister, and me—Barbara and I enjoyed my parents' company. Despite our unconventional lifestyle and my dogged insistence on questioning certain of their assumptions, I think they enjoyed ours.

When we had to move my parents from the mountain home where they had both believed they would live out their years to a retirement community more appropriate to their needs, much of the fabric began to unravel. As a requisite to figuring capital gains tax, I had to know what they once paid for land, architectural plans, and the original construction of their house. My research revealed that each had cost almost twice the family myth; my parents' frequently repeated figures had been about half of what they had actually paid.

Why this halving of such expenditures? Was it to maintain the appearance of having less? Was it that they wanted to be seen as having gotten a better deal than they actually did? Were they still ashamed of unearned wealth? Did they fear being taken advantage of if people knew what they had? All of these. And perhaps they were right. Some who did know certainly used the information against them. When I'd learned enough to understand, I could clearly see that a dishonest broker, for example, had bought and sold Dad's stocks when he wanted a commission, not when such trading would have been advantageous to his client.

It has taken me a while, but I now recognize signs of similar breaches in myself: pretending I've had less than I had, or saying I'd acquired an item more cheaply than its actual price. What about the expensive dress I once claimed to have bought on sale? A much smaller amount, but wasn't the nature of the lie the same, motivated by similar distortions where money is concerned? What of the six-thousand-dollar hot tub and deck I once told people cost me four? I didn't want my friends to think me extravagant. And yes, I also wanted them to praise me for having obtained such a bargain.

Feminist theory and memory work has helped to make such lies superfluous. Observing my parents' lives has helped me strengthen a self-esteem that no longer needs these lies. But money is something like food, in that we need it to survive, and so total abstinence is also not the answer. People with eating disorders are constantly running into the dilemma: we cannot give up eating as others might give up drinking or smoking or using drugs. I'm not suggesting a pecking order of difficulty here. I'm just saying that when the dis-ease thrives around something with which we must come in contact many times a day, healing may require a different process. Going back to the root is imperative.

I ponder the role money played in the various primary relationships I've had. My first husband came from a wealthy family. We were hardly more than children; neither of us had a profession when we married. But I gladly stopped studying so that he might continue school. The traditional fifties. It seemed so much more important for him to graduate—a man who couldn't yet figure out what he wanted to do—than for me, who knew I would be a writer, to continue my education. I would be taken care of, just as my parents predicted. Or I would make it *look* like I was being taken care of.

Oh how difficult it was to let go of that facade, and how humiliating!

After we divorced, I went to New York where I worked at odd jobs, honed my writing skills, believed all else was secondary. When I decided to have a child, everything changed. Supporting two is much more than twice the work of supporting one, particularly when the additional mouth to feed is a child's. Ask any single mother. It also sheds a whole new light on the word responsibility. From then on I nurtured myself as principal provider. The two fathers of my second, third, and fourth children rarely took that job on in any consistent or dependable way.

I say that I *nurtured* my provider role, because I am aware that this was, at least unconsciously, a decision. Of course I was conditioned, as all women are. But again, it was about control, about exercising unhealthy control when I couldn't find my way to the healthy variety. My partners frequently had trouble seeing themselves as responsible for our children's welfare. And I gained effusive praise in my "martyrdom." This wasn't only about money, but about attending to the children, dealing with housework, all the invisible and repetitive tasks that keep a family going. Especially once we were no longer together, getting child support went from difficult to impossible.

I accepted the role of only or primary earner. I remembered the relative ease of having had my son on my own: no cross-currents of contrasting child rearing philosophies. Providing economically as well as emotionally for one, two, three, and then four children wasn't easy, but I was in control. And, I told myself, the children weren't being pulled in different directions.

With my last male partners, and later when I began to live with women, our economic balance or imbalance would be reflective of another period in my life. Now my children were grown. Only the youngest still needed some help with her education. I was able to conceive of a different sort of relationship to money, one in which I might begin to do some of the things I had longed for, most importantly make writing time central. I could also try to design some security as I aged in a capitalist system that is so little responsive to human need. Still, my patterns had been set over time. I continued to manipulate my children and others through money misuse.

Barbara and I have been together for almost ten years. She came into the relationship out of a working-class background, an artist who then earned her living painting signs. She lived modestly, had almost no money put aside, and described this as her choice. She didn't want to be burdened with unnecessary baggage, she said—liked the freedom to pick up and go. From an upper-middle-class family and with many more years of professional experience, I had more in the way of potential funding, but lacked some very specific skills.

For one thing, I had lived outside the United States for almost a quarter century. Returning in my late forties, I had no job, was without a credit rating, and didn't have the most elemental knowledge about money management in a society like ours. Then, almost immediately, I found myself in the middle of a high-profile political battle for the right to remain in the country of my birth. When Barbara and I got together, my immigration case was raging.

Upon my return to the United States, I looked at teaching as something I might be suited for; it seemed to me that I had a great deal to share and I knew the college classroom would also be an excellent place from which to tap the pulse of this country I had left so many years before. Much was familiar but much had changed. I did manage to get teaching jobs, first as an adjunct and then as a visiting professor, at a number of schools.

Although I never achieved tenured employment, teaching was always a wonderful experience. I loved the interaction with my students. I also quickly learned how women, minorities, radicals, and anyone who is perceived of as different are used and abused on college campuses—what it means to have benefits one day and none the next—how difficult it is to keep health insurance in one's fifties and without a retirement plan. I heard colleagues' stories of what they had to go through to get tenure, saw excellent female professors lose out because they weren't considered "congenial" (a criterion rarely applied to men). I began to understand firsthand that there is little difference in how a rapidly computerizing society treats its teachers from how it treats its auto workers or service personnel. Only the myths are different.

Perhaps because I had experienced working and raising my children in a socialist society (Cuba) as well as one that was politically and economically innovative (Nicaragua during the Sandinista eighties), I returned to the United States with a broader sense of the possibilities inherent in differing economies. I knew it was about priorities; a healthy population should be valued above an exaggerated defense. What I lacked in street smarts, I probably made up for in the freshness of my gaze. Everything was open to question; I took little for granted. And I was curious about how someone like myself might earn a living, buy time to write, and design an old age that would not be a burden to others, particularly the woman I came to love, who is 16 years younger than I.

Working while under threat of deportation was itself a challenge. The law seemed to allow it while my case wound its way through the courts, and then again it did not. Changing legislation often brought my rights into contradictory focus. Eventually my hometown university closed its doors to me, and for eight years I taught at colleges that required my being away from home for five months out of every year.

At a certain point Barbara decided to go back to school and get a teaching certificate. My parents, good friends, and I all helped support her decision. This precipitated a shift in our relationship, particularly its economics. For the first time in my adult life I was looking at a situation in which I would not be the principal breadwinner for my immediate family. Older and exhausted from many years of such responsibility, I longed to write full time. It was also becoming more and more painful for Barbara and me to live apart for almost half of every year. When she began to teach we decided I could quit, that I would earn what I could from reading and lecturing while concentrating on my writing and photography.

This has meant much more than cutting back on a lifestyle that included frequent travel and other amenities. It has meant, for the first time in 58 years, not perceiving of myself as the one who must "do it all." It's about a new sense of time, but it's also about control: how to relinquish and also maintain it. Slowly, as our trust in one another built, Barbara and I merged assets, responsibilities, a common future.

I had to know, beyond words, that Barbara saw my children as family. I had to know that their future, and our contributions to it, was as important to her as it is to me. Early in our relationship she had her car, I mine. Gradually the cars were placed in both our names. Then the part we own of the house in which we live. Finally our bank accounts. We learned to talk to one another about what felt right and what didn't.

What does the talking sound like? Or, more importantly, what do the silences obscure? We both still have a tendency to do what we call secret clothes buying, that is, buying or ordering something without telling the other, who then discovers it in the closet we share. Shame at wanting more than we need? Probably. Barbara says she also feels uncomfortable when she breakfasts out; she can't rid herself of the fear that I will find this extravagant (which I don't).

Perhaps the most interesting way in which I continue to display my unhealthy attitudes about money is not with my children, who will no longer allow it, but with my mother, who depends on me for much of her emotional well-being as well as for the mechanics of handling her affairs. Because I have been angry for so long at what I see as Mother's self-absorption and inability to think creatively about her life, because I have tried to talk about the contradictions and gotten nowhere, and surely *because I am now the one in control,* I am unduly hard on this woman I love, about her apparent disinterest in learning anything about her finances.

My mother has told me that I intimidate her. This horrifies me, and I link it to our attitudes around money. "No," she insists, "it's because you know so much. Who wouldn't be intimidated by you?" Heartbroken, I am convinced we will never confront the real issues.

And life stumbles on.

As a much more recent participant, Barbara sees the larger picture more clearly than I; she also has less emotional investment. So she will point out that it wasn't really necessary for me to question Mom's eating all her lunches out. To tell her that if she wants to travel as much as she does, she'll have to curtail her extremely meager spending—or to scoff when she asks if she can afford a thrift-shop blouse costing $3.00 and then berate her for canceling a $31.00 subscription to the daily paper. "It's not necessary to confuse her," Barbara will remind me, "and anyway, it's not about any of that."

Not only coming to terms with our own attitudes about money, but learning to change them when necessary, is something Barbara and I do together; just as we encourage one another to eat right, get enough exercise, or deal with our other demons. I believe that our decisions are the product of principled feminism, cultivated trust, and a deep love.

But with money, as with almost all else, one is ultimately alone with one's ghosts. As a woman in my late fifties, as a lesbian, as an artist still learning how to value my own work while inhabiting a world in which money remains a metaphor for worth and control, when I am able to believe in myself I hope for a publisher's advance or an NEA. When I slip back into that inherited lack of self-confidence, I tend to place my bets on the Publisher's Clearinghouse variety of luck.

> Nana Jo thinks the hens are a nuisance: such clucking and filth. The eggs are nice, of course, and they make good conversation, so much larger than those the grocery boy delivers. One intrigued her with its bloody yoke. Another with two yokes became a story to tell. . . .
>
> He came home late again last night, smelling of something she

can't identify. She tries to find out, but a dreamy smile is all she gets. He doesn't seem interested in her anymore, not the way he was at first. She's never really liked his manicured attentions; perhaps she's made that clear, in spite of her best resolve. But she longs to feel wanted. And she wants others to know that she is wanted. She wishes he would reach out, even just so she could push his hand away.

And then there are his crazy expenditures: a thousand baby fir trees: who *needs* a thousand trees . . . the boat they'd enjoy—or *he'd* enjoy—until he tires of its novelty . . . an extra bathroom in the stable . . . yet another camera. . . .

"Will you look at this lens!" His face is strangely flushed. A rare excitement. "What do you want it for," she asks. She isn't looking at him, but raises her eyebrows and glances to see the reaction on her daughter's face.

"If you don't change, I'm going to go out and sell eggs," she threatens. "Door to door. What do you think our neighbors will say about us then?"

He smiles before he turns away.

Notes

CHAPTER 1 **Money Talk, or The Last Frontier**

1. In *Bridges, A Journal for Jewish Feminists and our Friends*, Volume 2, Number 1, Spring 1991, 5751.

2. By 1989, only 27% of all households in the United States conformed to the traditional nuclear family (i.e., a married couple with children under 18). This is a decrease from 74% in 1960. "For some women [supporting their families alone is] a choice, facilitated by greater economic indepen-dence and increasing social acceptance. For others, especially African American women, [it is] also the result of a shortage of men caused primarily by high death and incarceration rates. Whatever the reason, over the past 30 years, the share of households maintained by a woman (includ-ing families, unrelated individuals living together, and people living alone) has grown rapidly, from 18% in 1960 to 28% in 1990." *Statistical Abstract* 1990, 45, 48. In *Race Gender & Work: A Multicultural Economic History of Women in the United States* by Teresa L. Amott and Julie A. Matthaei (Boston: South End Press, 1991), 310–311.

3. This quote is from one of my narrators, a Jewish woman of working-class origin who became a tenured professor at a large university. She is active, among many other areas, in anti-racist work.

Notes

4. From "Subject to Debate," in *The Nation*, by Katha Pollitt, February 1995.

5. This may be changing. There are disturbing trends, like that exemplified by the recent Michigan decision in which a judge awarded child custody to a father because the mother—who had raised the child—had put her in daycare in order to pursue a college education which would clearly benefit both mother and child in the long run. The father wouldn't care for his child either, but *his* mother would. This, the judge said, offered the child a more stable home environment.

6. From "Many Rivers to Cross" in *On Call* by June Jordan (Boston: South End Press, 1985), 20.

7. The U.S. Bureau of the Census (1994) shows women's life expectancy at birth as 79 years, compared to 73 for men. Figures are higher in some countries—Japan's is 82 to 76—and much lower in others—Zimbabwe shows 44 to 40—but globally, women consistently outlive men. Among poor people of color and whites in the inner-city ghettos, men are more prone to early death from street violence, a phenomenon that also widens the gap.

CHAPTER 2 The Almighty Dollar, or The Popular Culture of Money

1. The motto first appeared on U.S. coins in 1864, during the divisive and difficult years of our country's Civil War. In 1908, Roosevelt's Congress passed a law requiring that "In God We Trust" appear on all coins. In 1955, Eisenhower signed legislation extending use of the motto to paper currency; this was implemented in 1957. *The Secret Life of Money, Teaching Tales of Spending, Receiving, Saving, and Owing* by Tad Crawford (New York: G.P. Putnam's Sons, 1994), 34–36.

2. Wright built The First National Bank in Dwight, Illinois in 1905. It still stands at 122 West Street. His City National Bank and Hotel was built in Mason City, Iowa, in 1909. It is now called Adams Building and Park Inn, and is at the corner of West State Street and South Federal Avenue. Both of these edifices were designed to evoke our culture's worship of money. *Buildings by Frank Lloyd Wright in Seven Middle Western States 1887–1959* by Burnham Library of Architecture (Chicago: Art Institute of Chicago, 1963.)

3. Crawford, *The Secret Life of Money*.

4. Crawford, *The Secret Life of Money*, 12.

5. LETS was started in 1983 in the Comox Valley of British Columbia and

has become a model for other such community currency experiments throughout Canada and the United States.

6. Quoted in "The Potential of Local Currencies" by Susan Meeker-Lowry in *Z Magazine*, Boston, July/August 1995, 16–23.

7. Ibid., 16.

8. "The Psychology of Money" by James Buchan, in *Granta* 49, Fall 1994, London, 100.

9. *The Secret Life of Money* by Tad Crawford, 16.

10. *Howl* by Allen Ginsberg (San Francisco: City Lights Books, 1956), 17–18.

11. The Wheel of Fortune is one of the country's most popular game shows, broadcast each weeknight on CBS. Contestants spin a large wheel divided into spaces representing sums of money, bankruptcy, the loss of a turn, or a surprise item. Where the wheel stops then gives or denies the contestant a turn at contributing a letter to a phrase on a large lighted board. The participant who "earns" the most money while successfully deciphering the round of puzzles wins.

12. Estimated diamond sales in the United States in 1994 were $13 billion, an all-time high and a 7% increase over the previous year. The diamond engagement ring market alone was valued at $2.6 billion. The average price of an engagement ring was $1,600, representing an average of two month's salary to the man who purchased one. Still, 76% of all new brides will wear a diamond. (Data from American Diamond Industry Association, Diamond Information Center, and National Family Opinion Poll. *U.S. News and World Report*, May 22, 1955, 18).

13. One hundred sixty, according to an item on ABC evening news, February 11, 1995.

14. "How You Can Save Wall Street" in *The Worst Years of Our Lives* by Barbara Ehrenreich, 220–221.

15. "How to Help the Uptrodden" in *The Worst Years of Our Lives* by Barbara Ehrenreich, 230.

CHAPTER 4 **From Shame to Resistance: The Money Lies**

1. Sue Doro has written an extraordinary essay about her life which appears as "Focus" in *Liberating Memory, Our Work and Our Working Class Consciousness*, edited and with an introduction by Janet Zandy (Rutgers University Press: New Brunswick, New Jersey, 1995), 37–53.

CHAPTER 5 **The Wealthy Woman: Money versus Power**

1. "The Masculinization of Wealth" by Gloria Steinem, in *Moving Beyond Words* (New York: Simon & Schuster, 1994), 175–196.

2. Steinem, *Moving Beyond Words*, 182–183.

3. Idem, 187.

4. *Passion and Prejudice* by Sallie Bingham (New York: Applause Books, 1989), 487.

5. Women of color who used their money in this way were less likely to make it into the history books than white women with similar missions. See Michelle Cliff's novel *Free Enterprise* (New York: Dutton, 1993) for a fictionalized but nonetheless accurate account of Pleasant's work.

6. Resourceful Women: 3543 18th Street, #9, San Francisco, California 94110, (415) 431–5677, FAX (415) 431–9634.

7. "Women's giftgiving—the philosophy of the Foundation for a Compassionate Society," by Genevieve Vaughan, xeroxed copy distributed at the Michigan Women's Music Festival, 1994.

8. Bingham, *Passion and Prejudice*, xv.

9. Steinem, *Moving Beyond Words*, 195.

10. Bingham, *Passion and Prejudice*, xvi.

11. "Philanthropy: Do 'Universal' Dollars Reach Women and Girls," a special report from The National Council for Research on Women, *Issues Quarterly*, Volume 1, Number 2, p. 9. This and following data is from *Foundation Giving Yearbook of Facts and Figures: Private, Corporate and Community Foundations* (New York: Foundation Center, 1994). The National Council for Research on Women is at 530 Broadway at Spring Street, 10th floor, New York, NY 10012–3920.

12. Steinem, *Moving Beyond Words*, 188.

13. *Fragments: My Path Through the 20th Century* by Kit Tremaine (Nevada City, California: Blue Dolphin Press, 1992), 10.

14. Bingham, *Passion and Prejudice*, xii.

15. Bingham, *Passion and Prejudice*, xiii.

16. "Such and such is as such and such does" is patiently repeated by Gump throughout the film whenever he is faced with a question or situation that momentarily challenges his meager intellect. It is his memory of his mother's first advice: "Smart is as smart does."

CHAPTER 6 **How We Change, or Some Alternatives to Money as Power**

1. For an exercise in cost-sharing, women break up into small groups to talk about their economic situations and how much they believe they can contribute to whatever event or organizational endeavor is being planned. Members of the groups, who have engaged in the necessary research, detail the cost. Throughout the process, space is made for questions, decisions about how much each woman feels she wants to contribute, and reconnecting with other women from one's background/situation as well as with those who have pledged in one's general range. Besides imbuing the organization of a particular activity with a greater degree of fairness—who supports the endeavor and how—this sort of process gives women of different economic means the opportunity of talking with those like themselves who pledged more, those like themselves who pledged less, and those unlike themselves who pledged the same amount, all in a spirit of honest questioning and challenge. ("Coming Out About Money: Cost Sharing Across Class Lines" by Felice Yeskel, in *Bridges*, Spring/Summer 1992, 102–114.)

2. *Bridges, A Journal for Jewish Feminists and Our Friends*, Volume 4, Number 2, Winter 94/95, 4–5.

3. "The Potential of Local Currency" by Susan Meeker-Lowry in *Z Magazine*, July/August 1995, 16–23.

4. Susan Meeker-Lowry quotes *New Money for Healthy Communities* by Thomas Greco.

CHAPTER 7 **The Egg Route**

1. I lived outside the country—in Mexico, Cuba, and Nicaragua—from 1961 to 1984. During that time I developed a progressive political outlook and activism and wrote a number of books in which I expressed views critical of U.S. government policy, particularly in Southeast Asia and Central America. In 1967, married to a Mexican and with three young children to support, I took out Mexican citizenship. It was not a political act, but economic, an effort to find better work in a time of need. Almost two decades later, and back in my country of birth, this made it possible for the U.S. Immigration and Naturalization Service to attempt to deport me under one of the clauses of the infamous 1952 McCarran-Walter Act. My writings were judged subversive. The case, which I fought (and won in 1989), cost a quarter of a million dollars, money raised by New York City's Center for Constitutional Rights through direct appeal, house parties, benefit concerts, bowl-a-thons, read-ins, and many other creative campaigns.

Notes

2. Haydeé Santamaría was one of the two women involved from the beginning in Fidel Castro's 26th of July Movement. She was imprisoned after the 1953 attack on Moncada Barracks, the first military operation of the then fledgling organization. Later she was active in exile and with the guerrilla forces in the mountains. When the revolution came to power she held a number of important posts, among them President of Casa de las Américas, one of Cuba's prominent cultural institutions. She was also a member of the Cuban Communist Party's Central Committee until her death by suicide in 1980. Haydeé often spoke of a society in which all differences would be a thing of the past and everyone would have access to all they needed—very much including the needs of the spirit.